BESS OF HARDWICK
1527-1608

First published in 2001 by
Short Books Ltd
15 Highbury Terrace
London N5 1UP

A CIP catalogue record for this book
is available from the British Library.

ISBN 0 571 20800 2

Printed in Great Britain by
Bookmarque Ltd, Croydon, Surrey

A MATERIAL GIRL
BESS OF HARDWICK
1527-1608

KATE HUBBARD

✳ SHORT BOOKS

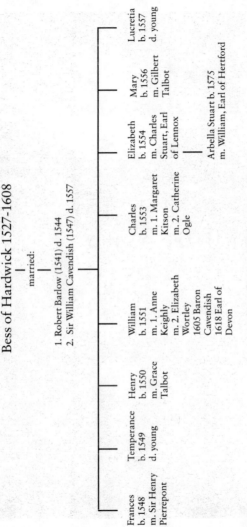

Bess of Hardwick 1527–1608

married:

1. Robert Barlow (1541) d. 1544
2. Sir William Cavendish (1547) d. 1557
3. Sir William St Loe (1559) d. 1565
4. George Talbot, Earl of Shrewsbury (1567) d. 1590

Frances
b. 1548
m. Sir Henry
Pierrepont

Temperance
b. 1549
d. young

Henry
b. 1550
m. Grace
Talbot

William
b. 1551
m. 1. Anne
Keighly
m. 2. Elizabeth
Wortley
1605 Baron
Cavendish
1618 Earl of
Devon

Charles
b. 1553
m. 1. Margaret
Kitson
m. 2. Catherine
Ogle

Elizabeth
b. 1554
m. Charles
Stuart, Earl
of Lennox

Arbella Stuart b. 1575
m. William, Earl of Hertford

Mary
b. 1556
m. Gilbert
Talbot

Lucretia
b. 1557
d. young

IT TOOK 23 LABOURERS four weeks to dig and lay the foundations of Hardwick New Hall in November 1590. Breaking through to the bedrock of a bleak and wind-swept Derbyshire hilltop, they set in motion the great organisational engine required to construct a 16th-century house. Materials had been accumulated – stone quarried, timber felled, sawpits dug, limestone burned. Skilled and much sought-after craftsmen had been hired and an overseer of the building appointed. By the end of December, the 'fleaks', or hurdles, which formed a rudimentary scaffolding for the ground floor, were in place. As Shakespeare began work on his first play, *Henry VI*, Hardwick's walls rose.

For Elizabeth, Countess of Shrewsbury, later known as Bess of Hardwick, the start of these building works brought the realisation of a long-held dream. In that same November she had buried her fourth husband, George Talbot, Earl of Shrewsbury, and with him years of marital harassment. Now an immensely wealthy widow in her mid-sixties, she found herself free to devote her still considerable energy to the passion that had shaped and animated her life – the building of the most beautiful house in Elizabethan England.

Today, Hardwick graces the Derbyshire skyline, its masses of golden stone shifting before the eye, its expanses of diamond-paned glass glittering in the sunlight, its turrets crowned by giant ES's. Bess's identity is stamped, quite literally, all over the house; not just outside but in, where, like the doodling of a monstrous child, her initials are carved into overmantels and embroidered on cushions, tapestries and hangings. At once romantic and austere, ostentatious and restrained, of its time and forward-looking, it is a building whose compact, regular exterior belies the ingenious use of interior space, whose contradictions reflect the foibles and preferences of its builder. Hardwick stands not only as a monument to a brilliantly managed marital and business career, it also celebrates one woman's triumphant survival and proclaims her desire for immortality. It would have brought a smile to Bess's thin lips to know that she would become synonymous with a house not a husband.

This Derbyshire squire's daughter set her sights high. With the spirit of an adventuress and the heart of a shop-keeper, she forged a path through the Elizabethan world, leaving four husbands, four houses and a scattering of enemies in her wake. Bess enjoyed a long and for the most part cordial association with the Queen (Elizabeth I, with little love of women and wives in particular, perhaps recognised in Bess someone of her own mettle) only jeopardised by her schemes to set a grandchild on the English throne. She was a close friend of such powers at Court as Lord Burghley and the Earl of Leicester, the Queen's chief adviser and favourite respectively, and within the larger arena of Elizabethan society she was highly respected and probably feared. As the wife of the Earl of Shrewsbury, who was appointed jailor to Mary Queen of Scots in 1568, she found herself housing a recalcitrant royal prisoner for 16 long years. Partly as a consequence, her marriage to Shrewsbury broke down in a spectacularly bitter and public manner, providing Elizabethans with a running soap opera and a rare instance of Bess losing control of events.

By 1600 she commanded an annual income of around £20,000, making her the richest woman in England (only superseded by the Queen, whose revenues stood at £300,000) and presided over a vast acreage of land from Derbyshire to Gloucestershire. She provided a much used moneylending service, dipping into the coffers stacked about her bed at Hardwick, for loans – at competitive rates naturally – to impoverished members of the nobility. And she built compulsively: apart from Hardwick New Hall, Bess was responsible for Hardwick Old Hall (this stands today, a ruin, beside the New), the original house at Chatsworth and a house, called Oldcotes, for her son, William Cavendish. No other woman in Britain, before or since, has built on such a scale.

Hers, of course, was an age of great builders – an age of enterprise. William Harrison, an Essex clergyman, in 1577 described how every English builder 'desireth to set his house aloft on the hill, to be seen afar off, and cast forth his beames of stately and curious workmanship into every quarter of the country'. Ability, combined with ambition and, crucially, royal favour, made fortunes, which were proclaimed and displayed in the glorious houses that sprang up all over England. Most of their builders were, like Bess, culturally ignorant and certainly unfamiliar with the principles of Renaissance architecture (the Renaissance, as an intellectual movement, barely touched 16th-century England), but some of its features, symmetrical design or classical ornamentation, both of which were employed at Hardwick, were borrowed by patrons and their craftsmen as architectural frills to be grafted on to an indigenous Gothic tradition. Elizabethan houses fire the imagination precisely because of their eclecticism, their lack of allegiance to any single architectural school or controlling mind, the magpie spirit with which their builders adopted and adapted.

Although of more modest dimensions than a 'Prodigy House' – the extraordinarily lavish constructions built by courtiers to entertain the Queen, who had adroitly passed the building baton on to her subjects – Bess intended Hardwick to dazzle, to stand as a showcase for those features so coveted by Elizabethan builders: symmetry, architectural 'devices' and glass. To give shape to her vision, she engaged the services of a man who had worked on some of the most exuberant, inventive and romantic houses to be found in 16th-century England, who came close to occupying the position of 'architect' at a time, predating the advent of Inigo Jones, when such a term had no currency and little meaning: Robert Smythson.

Smythson produced a simple but ingenious 'platt' (plan) for Hardwick, based on a Greek cross – a rectangle surrounded by six turrets, two on each long and one on each short side. Sacheverell Sitwell, one of the house's great admirers, described how these turrets mysteriously regroup themselves according to the position from which they are viewed – 'as though the building is shaped like a diamond on a playing card, more still, like the ace of clubs, so that the fourth tower is hidden, almost, behind the other three'. This kind of optical illusion is an instance of an Elizabethan 'device', a trick or invention designed to amaze. Devices went beyond the architectural, they could be literary – as in the sonnet – or they could apply to the wider arena of the personal and the political, the pervasive love of intrigue that animated the Elizabethan world and would prove irresistible to Bess.

Two unusual features of Smythson's 'platt', whereby symmetry and glass are displayed to maximum effect, seem to betray Bess's hand. Just as in her previous house, Hardwick Old Hall, the servants' hall runs crossways, not, as in medieval houses, lengthways, and the staterooms are on the second floor rather than the first. Correspondingly, Hardwick's windows increase rather than diminish in height, as they rise, storey by storey. Elizabethans were keenly aware of the importance of the internal approach, the sense of expectation and drama that could build within a house. Lord Burghley wrote to Sir Christopher Hatton about Sir Cristopher's house, Holdenby: 'I found nothing of greater grace than your stately ascent from your hall to your great chamber, and your chamber answerable with largeness and lightsomeness.' Much the same could be said of Hardwick. Bess clearly loved light as she did height and she ensured that visitors, after they had wound their way up the wide, shallow stone stairs, would marvel at the soaring ceilings and windows of the great chamber and the long gallery.

They would also have marvelled at the sheer amount of glass. 'You shall sometimes have Faire Houses so full of Glasse, that one cannot tell where to become to be out of the Sunne or Cold,' wrote Sir Francis Bacon. Other Elizabethan houses – Sir John Thynne's Longleat, or Sir Francis Willoughby's Wollaton – gloried in large, expensive and status-enhancing windows, but 'Hardwick Hall more glass than wall' outdid them all.

If Bess built in the spirit of her times, as a materialist rather than an aesthete, her sex set her apart. Elizabethan women were expected to be passive, housebound creatures, tied to their embroidery. A 'Homily on Marriage', read in church every Sunday, designated the woman a 'weak creature not endued with like strength and constancy of mind'. In practice, of course, there were women who defied their husbands, and women who took an interest in their husbands' business affairs and building projects. But with her financial acumen, her success in not just retaining (under 16th-century law a woman's property, on marriage, was made over to her husband, and wives could not independently own freehold land) but multiplying her lands, and as the initiator and driving force behind four houses, Bess was unique.

Historians, especially 19th-century male historians, have demonised Bess, as a monster of overweening ambition and avarice, as a traitor to her sex. In 1883 Edmund Lodge, in *Illustrations of British History*, summed her up as: 'A woman of masculine understanding and conduct, proud, furious, selfish and unfeeling. She was a builder, a buyer and seller of estates, a moneylender, a farmer and a merchant of lead, coals and timber; when disengaged from these employments she intrigued alternately with Elizabeth and Mary, always to the prejudice and terror of her husband.' To an extent he was right. Bess was immensely ambitious, not merely for her own interests but for those of her family, her children. When she believed those interests were threatened she was relentlessly litigious, but her sense of justice extended to those beneath her – she was a fair employer and she commanded loyalty in return. She could and did behave like a tyrant, but like many tyrants she cried easily. Towards her family, so long as she was unopposed, she was devoted and affectionate. She was unsentimental not 'unfeeling', though eminently capable of maintaining a tight rein on her own emotions, while provoking extremes in, if not permanently antagonising, those around her.

**

We know little of Bess during the early years, the years of obscurity. Sometime in the mid-1520s, and no later than 1527, while Henry VIII was attempting to rid himself of his first wife, Catherine of Aragon, Bess was born, in Derbyshire, in the original Hardwick. It was then a farmhouse, probably half-timbered, owned, along with 400 acres, by her father, John Hardwick, a Derbyshire squire. John Hardwick was married to Elizabeth Leake and they had five children – four daughters, of whom Bess was the second youngest, and a son. Bess's education as a country squire's daughter would have been rudimentary – reading, writing (she acquired an extremely distinctive hand: bold, slanting, and, most unusual among 16th-century correspondents, absolutely legible), basic maths, embroidery. As an adult she had little or no intellectual interests; her bedside reading at Hardwick consisted of three pious volumes: Calvin on Job, Solomon's Proverbs and a book of meditations.

In 1528 John Hardwick died, leaving his widow and children in precarious financial circumstances. This was thanks to the iniquitous Tudor system of wardship, whereby an estate, if the heir was under 21, became Crown property, administered by the Court of Wards, until the heir came of age. He, or she, became a ward, with a guardian who bought the wardship and who could then arrange the ward's marriage, and hence the future of the property, as he saw fit. Since little James Hardwick was only a year old, the Court of Wards took over the estate. Elizabeth Hardwick's only option was to take a second husband, which she did in the person of Ralph Leche, a local man, with whom she had three more daughters. Marriage was Bess's only option too, and not an easy matter considering that all she had was a dowry of

40 marks (or £33) left her by her father.

Rachel Lloyd, housekeeper at Kensington Palace and a friend of Countess Spencer, whose daughter Georgiana married Bess's descendant, the 5th Duke of Devonshire, wrote an admiring memoir of Bess in the 18th century, marvelling at her ability 'to rise by every husband into greater wealth and higher honours'. Those husbands were chosen carefully, as sound investments, though Bess had a far better head for business than any of them; yet she clearly had sufficient charm, as well as, reputedly, beauty and wit (the latter is admittedly not to the fore in her letters) to ensnare them in the first place.

She could not have been more than 14 when she married the equally youthful Robert Barlow. According to Nathaniel Johnson, who wrote an account of Bess in 1692 and heard the story from 'some ancient Gentlemen', the couple met in London, at the house of a Lady Zouch, where Robert, who was also from Derbyshire, lay sick with 'Chronical Distemper' and Bess 'being very sollicitous to afford him all the help she was able to do in his sickness, ordering his diet and attendance, being then young and very handsome, he fell deeply in love with her'.

Johnson is not the most reliable of chroniclers, but the substance of the story is probably true. Penniless girls were commonly taken into the households of wealthy relatives and Lady Zouch was distantly related to the

Hardwicks. Whether or not it was a love-match, it was of short duration and possibly unconsummated. Margaret, Duchess of Newcastle, in her 'Life of William Duke of Newcastle' – Bess's grandson – wrote that Robert Barlow 'died [in 1544] before they were bedded together, they both being very young'.

According to Elizabethan law, a widow received one third of her husband's estate, for life. In practice this was far from straightforward. Bess's inheritance, her widow's 'jointure', amounted to a modest £8.15s annually, but because Robert Barlow had been under-age his estate passed into the hands of the Court of Wards and her jointure became the subject of years of legal wrangling, not settled until 1553. Aged 18 or 19, she had discovered that the rights of the widow were far superior to those of the wife, but that given the impossibly complex legal system they frequently needed to be fought for. These early years of financial insecurity and loss help to explain Bess's drive to fortify herself with land, assets and cash (though no such drive manifested itself in her brother, James, who frittered away what money he had, found himself selling Hardwick to his sister and died a bankrupt in the Fleet prison). For Bess the process of acquisition became compulsive, not so much a matter of security as of power and control. Her dreams were large and they were centred on her birthplace – Hardwick, Derbyshire.

In the years following Robert Barlow's death Bess disappears from view. She may have become a lady-in-waiting to Lady Dorset. Certainly this would have thrown her in the path of the man who was to become her second husband, Sir William Cavendish, a friend of the Marquis of Dorset. In 1547, the year Henry VIII died and ten-year-old Edward VI succeeded to the throne, Sir William recorded in a notebook, 'Memorandum. That I was married unto Elizabeth Hardwick my third Wiffe in Leestersheere at Bradgate House the 20th August in the first yeare of Kinge Edward the 6 at 2 of the Clock after midnight.'

The Duchess of Newcastle wrote that Cavendish 'being somewhat advanced in years married her chiefly for her beauty'. A portrait of Bess in her thirties hangs at Hardwick, and shows her gazing benignly into the middle distance. Her cheeks are plump, her hair red, her eyes blue and rather small and her nose long. Her loose gown, worn over a bodice and skirt, is lined with soft white fur; the bodice sleeves are elaborately embroidered and there are enamelled bracelets on her wrists and pearls at her throat; a jewelled French hood (made fashionable by Anne Boleyn) sits on the back of her head. In her beringed, capable-looking hands she holds a pair of leather gloves, a mark of status. If hardly to modern eyes a great beauty, she looks every inch the prosperous young matron.

Bess's looks notwithstanding, Sir William found himself in the happy position of marrying a woman some 20 years his junior, yet one to whom he was temperamentally well suited. And if Bess loved any of her husbands it was most probably the cheerfully materialist Sir William, the father of her children, the husband whose ambitions she shared.

Like Bess, Cavendish came from the landed gentry, by far the most vigorous and dynamic class in socially mobile 16th-century England. He was the second son of a Suffolk squire, with no material advantages but plenty of energy and ability. He may have been a gentleman servant to Cardinal Wolsey, and he certainly grew rich under Henry VIII as a Commissioner for the Dissolution of the Monasteries. Cavendish was a man prepared to bow before the prevailing wind – a prerequisite for advancement at the Tudor Court – and tactfully embraced Catholicism when Mary I came to the throne. By 1546, he had ascended through the Court ranks to become Treasurer of the King's Chamber, a position which he bought for £1,000, and a Privy Councillor.

His rise was entirely typical of an age of which Lord Keynes wrote, 'Never in the annals of the modern world has there existed so prolonged and so rich an opportunity for the business man, the speculator and the profiteer.' Whilst the fortunes of the nobility were in decline, drained away by debt, widows' jointures and badly managed estates, for the gentry they were there for the making. Members of the yeomen and merchant classes passed into the ranks of the gentry, members of the gentry into those of the nobility. Sir William Cecil, made Lord Burghley by Elizabeth I in 1571 and her Lord High Treasurer soon after, was an example of the latter and so, of course, was Bess herself. What Bess brought with her were the traits of the gentry – prudence, pragmatism and the kind of rigour she applied to her household accounts. These can be read today at Chatsworth, volume after volume meticulously detailing a lifetime's transactions, kept by a clerk but totted up every two weeks by Bess and signed with her confident, slanting 'E Shrowesbury'. And it was precisely because she retained those traits (just as she retained her flat Derbyshire vowels) that she held on to her fortune.

Others fared less well. The Court was rife with self-made men sprung from obscurity, like Christopher Hatton, an unknown Northamptonshire gentleman who rose to prominence, becoming a knight and a member of the Privy Council thanks to little more than a handsome face and a nimble turn on the dance floor. Hatton, as it turned out, overreached himself by building Holdenby, the largest and grandest of all the Prodigy Houses, and leaving his heir, Sir William Hatton, with crippling debts, of which Bess would later take swift advantage, stepping in and buying Holdenby's tapestries for Hardwick.

In 1548 Bess gave birth to her first child, a girl, Frances, named after her friend Frances Grey (formerly Frances Brandon and now the wife of the Marquis of Dorset) and two years later to her first son, Henry, who was to become 'my bad son Henry', the source of much trouble and disappointment. As godparents the Cavendishes chose the Marquis of Dorset, the Earl of Warwick and, most gratifyingly of all, Princess Elizabeth, half-sister of Edward VI. It was the beginning of a long if sometimes strained association between Bess and the future Queen. Four more children survived, William, Charles, Elizabeth and Mary; two daughters, Temperance and Lucretia, died young.

The Cavendishes set themselves up in two properties, at Northaw in Hertfordshire and in a London house in the shadow of the towering spire (destroyed by lightning in 1561) of the old St Paul's. Here Bess had her first real taste of high life brought by wealth and royal favour. Her accounts, itemised daily in her own hand, reveal something of the business of 16th-century domesticity. One Friday in December she paid for a quarter of mutton, a quarter of veal, half a peck of flour, suet, a pint of cream, cinnamon, ginger, mace and cloves (a pudding must have been on the menu), a dozen sparrows, apples, currants, a pound of soap and seven pints of wine. The

Cavendishes consumed a range of foods only enjoyed by the rich: a diet heavy on meat (especially mutton and capons), fish (oysters, whiting, shrimps, eels, herrings and turbot) and small birds (larks and blackbirds). Vegetables featured little, though 'salad oil' indicates that 'sallats' were eaten ('sallats' were made of cooked and preserved, as well as raw vegetables, and were often decorated with flowers), and there was plenty of seasonal fruit: cherries, apples and pears. The household got through pounds of butter, which Elizabethans liked to flavour and eat as a side dish. Bess bought bread, from a bakery, as well as more exotic items imported from the Continent, such as oranges, lemons, dried fruits, salt and olives. There are regular payments for pints of wine and gallons of ale, milk for the children, coal and candles. Cloth was bought to make clothes and the family needed a vast number of new shoes. There are also incidental expenses – for the mending of a toasting fork, for the man who carved the meat, and for Bess's daughters to go and see the Queen.

In the evenings Bess and Sir William, who entertained regularly, liked to gamble, usually at cards, while drinking quantities of wine and ale, or a posset, which was a kind of 16th-century toddy, made of 'sack' – a white wine – mixed with milk and herbs. Judging from his portrait, Sir William was a man of large appetites. His shrewd eyes are lost in folds of florid flesh, his nose is bulbous, his walrus moustache and beard luxuriant; altogether he is of a distinctly bibulous and corpulent appearance which, given his daily intake of four pints of wine, is hardly surprising.

Sir William was said to be so enamoured of his young wife that he enthusiastically embraced her designs on Derbyshire. In 1549 the Cavendishes bought Chatsworth, a manor house with some land, for £600. In the following years they pursued a determined programme of buying surrounding land. A deal was made with the Crown whereby Sir William's Hertfordshire estates, including Northaw, were exchanged for Derbyshire land. The manor at Ashford, which would later provide Bess with black-stone for Hardwick, together with 8,000 acres, were bought from the Earl of Westmoreland. Other, smaller parcels of land were added in. These were cannily bought in the names of both Sir William and his wife, ensuring that in the event of Sir William dying and Henry, his heir, being under-age, they would come under the control not of the Court of Wards, but of Bess. While it is unlikely that Sir William, who may have been a fond husband but was no fool, would have pursued a policy that didn't make sound business sense, the impetus must have come from Bess. Chatsworth provided her not only with a foothold in Derbyshire but also with her first building project.

'Everie man almost is a builder', wrote William Harrison, in his *Description of England in Shakespeare's*

Youth, 'and he that hath bought any small parcell of ground, be it never so little, will not be quiet till he have pulled downe the old house (if anie were there standing) and set up a new after his own devise.' So it was with Bess and Sir William. In 1551 a mason called Roger Worthe was paid to draw up a plan for Chatsworth. In place of the dilapidated manor they had bought, the Cavendishes erected an extremely large, quadrangular and sumptuously furnished house. Bess wrote to Sir John Thynne at Longleat asking if he could 'spare me your plasterer that flowereth your hall'. He couldn't, but a good deal of barter and exchange, of information, advice and craftsmen, as well as competition, did go on between patrons.

Skilled craftsmen, like plasterers and masons, were in great demand, and tended to move about the country in groups, from site to site (hence the term 'freemason'). Men who worked on Chatsworth, such as the stonemason Thomas Accres, or the great plasterer and mason, Abraham Smith, would go on to Hardwick. When Bess wasn't in residence, she sent detailed instructions to her workforce. Her steward was told to 'Cause the floor in my bed chamber to be made even either with plaster, clay or lime, and all the windows where the glass is broken to be mended... Let the weaver make beer for me forthwith for my own drinking and your master, and see that I have good store of it, for if I lack either good beer or charcoal or wood, I will blame nobody as much as I will do you.'

Building work at Chatsworth was to continue and to preoccupy Bess for another 18 years, though it came to a temporary halt on the death of Sir William. In the same notebook that Sir William had noted the hour of his marriage to Bess, she sadly recorded that of the death of her husband: 'Memorandum. That Sir William Cavendyshe Knight my most deare and well beloved Husband departed this present Life of Mundaie being the 25th daie of October betwixt the Howers of 8 and 9 of the same daie at Night in the yeare of our Lord God 1557. On whose Soule I most humbly beseeche the Lord to have Mercy and Ridd mee and his poore Children out of our greate Misserie. Elizabeth Cavendysshe.'

She found herself a widow with six children, and two stepdaughters from one of Sir William's previous marriages, and with the added burden of an extremely large debt, incurred by her dead husband, hanging over her. A deficit had been discovered by the Lord High Treasurer in Sir William's accounts to the tune of £5,237. The Tudor Court was an entirely venal organisation. Court offices, such as Sir William's, were bought and low salaries were topped up in the form of perks – the pocketing of profits or the selling of patronage. Sir William and Bess's land-buying sprees and the building of Chatsworth had had to be funded from somewhere and Sir William, if not over-scrupulous, had done no more than many another Court official by diverting revenues. In pursuing the charge, Mary I (Bloody Mary), who had succeeded her half-brother, Edward VI, may simply have seized on an excuse to disgrace a courtier friendly with Princess Elizabeth. Sir William had pleaded ill-health and claimed that if forced to repay the debt he, his 'poor wife and mine innocent children' would be 'utterly undone, like to end our days in no small penury'. In the end, death had absolved him, saddling Bess with the debt. This could have been settled easily enough by selling off the Derbyshire lands, but she preferred other means. In 1558 Elizabeth I came to the throne and proved her friendship to Bess by making her a lady-in-waiting. While Bess mourned Sir William, she remained a pragmatist. Elizabeth's Court offered unrivalled opportunities for husband-hunting.

In 1559, after two years of widowhood, Bess married Sir William St Loe. St Loe was a middle-aged bachelor and, if not a greatly romantic figure, possessed of sterling qualities. He had proved himself a faithful servant to Elizabeth from the days when she was a princess and he a gentleman attendant. During Mary I's brief reign he had found himself in the Tower, along with Elizabeth, for his very tenuous connection to the Protestant rebellion led by Sir Thomas Wyatt. For such loyalty he had been rewarded – the Queen had made him her Captain of the Guard and

Chief Butler of England, posts which were accompanied by annuities but also required near-constant attendance at Court. Perhaps St Loe's chief attraction for Bess, though, was his possession of large tracts of land in Somerset and Gloucestershire. He enjoyed a comfortable £500 a year in income and he was besotted with his wife.

Bess, by now in her mid-thirties, was still handsome and, perhaps more importantly, brimming with the kind of vigour and vitality that were lacking in the bachelor St Loe. His surviving letters to Bess are syrupy with endearments and longing: 'My owne more dearer to me than I am to myself… I pray you as you love me, let me shortly hear from you for the quieting of my unquiet mind, how your own sweet self and all yours do.' He escaped from Court when he could to visit Bess at Chatsworth with her children, but his truancy was not well received by the Queen, who had scant sympathy for wifely demands.

He wrote to Bess, after a particularly frosty royal reception: 'The Queen hath found great fault with my long absence, saying she would talk with me further and that she would well chide me. Whereunto I answered that when her Highness understood the truth and the cause, she would not be offended. Whereunto she said, "Very well, very well." Howbeit hand of hers I did not kiss.' He signed himself, 'Your loving husband with aching heart until we meet.' He sent her presents from London, such as a bone grace (a hair ornament) 'of the new ffassion'. Bess was possibly pining rather less, preoccupied as she was with the building at Chatsworth, which had resumed with the injection of funds from St Loe. 'My honest sweet Chatsworth', her husband addressed her in another letter, indicating he knew where her heart lay.

St Loe also obligingly settled the matter of William Cavendish's £5,237 debt by paying a fine of £1,000. He proved himself to be a model of generosity, taking on not just Bess's substantial financial requirements, but those of her children too. He provided a dowry for her step-daughter, Ann Cavendish, and he paid for Henry and William Cavendish to go to Eton, a modest 19s per term.

Trouble threatened Sir William and his Lady in the shape of Edward St Loe, Sir William's younger brother. Edward was a rogue. Some years earlier he had married a Mrs Scutt, who was said to be 'by nature a verye lustye yonge woman'. The very lusty young woman had been married to the very elderly Mr Scutt, who had died aged 90, seemingly poisoned by Edward. However, within a mere two months of marriage to Edward, Mrs Scutt had herself fallen victim to poison. A preferable candidate, it appeared, had caught Edward's eye, a woman intended as a bride for his brother William. Greed lay behind such skulduggery – Edward's dread of seeing the St Loe lands dispersed among his brother's heirs. He failed, though, to prevent Sir William marrying Bess and drawing up a will leaving her the 'Western Lands'. Sir William later denied any pressure on Bess's part, but these lands could only have been a welcome addition to her portfolio.

For Edward it was a most unwelcome development and before long he was dispensing the poison once again. While he was visiting the St Loes in London in 1561, both Sir William and Bess fell ill. Rumours flew. Edward St Loe was never accused, but three probably innocent men were sent to the Tower. One of these, Hugh Draper, a Bristol neighbour of Edward, was charged with having a 'conjurer or sorcerer practise matter against Sir William St Loe and my Ladie'. Margaret, Lady St Loe, William and Edward's mother, knew better, writing to Bess, 'I was sure you were poisoned when I was at London, and if you had not had a present remedy you had died... This was the good will he bear you when he came up to London to see you, as he said was none other cause his coming, which I know the contrary, for he liked nothing your marriage...'

That was not the last of Edward St Loe, who made a final attempt to destroy his brother's marriage by turning the tables and accusing Bess herself of trying to poison her husband. Sir William vigorously refuted the allegations, and indeed poisoning was not Bess's style. There seems no reason to suggest that she would have wished to rid herself of a husband who had shown himself to be unfailingly generous and biddable. Nevertheless, if she did, Sir William obliged, for by 1565 he was dead.

Bess now found herself a third-time widow, in possession of St Loe's 'Western Lands', the Cavendish estates, the magnificent Chatsworth and an annual income of about £1,600. These were assets which considerably upped the ante in the marriage market, as she well knew. Rather than retiring to Derbyshire to lead the life of a wealthy widow, she came to Court, probably as one of the Queen's Ladies of the Privy Chamber. But wealth brought notoriety and Bess soon found herself the target of gossip. Henry Jackson, a former tutor to her sons, started spreading scurrilous rumours, possibly connected with the circumstances of St Loe's death. They were taken seriously enough for the Queen to step in and the case to be brought before the High Commission. In a letter to the Archbishop of Canterbury, the Queen referred to Jackson's slander and requested the Commissioners 'to proceed to extreme punishment, by corporal or otherwise, openly or privately', so that Bess might be 'restored to her good name'. It isn't known what Jackson's 'extreme punishment' involved.

Other rumours concerned Bess's next match. As one courtier speculated, 'Either Lord Darcy or Sir John

Thynne shall marry my Lady St Loe, but not Harry Cobham.' In fact she had a better prize in her sights, the immensely rich George Talbot, Earl of Shrewsbury, whom she married in 1567, a matter of months after the death of his first wife. Years later Shrewsbury would write to her, 'When you were defamed and to the world a byword when you were St Loe's widow, I covered the imperfections by my intermarriage with you and brought you to all the honour you have and most of the wealth you now enjoy.' By then the Earl had come to believe Bess capable of any kind of infamy.

***

The Earl of Shrewsbury was a Midlands magnate, with a sheaf of properties: Sheffield Manor, Sheffield Castle, Wingfield Manor, Rufford Abbey, Welbeck Abbey, Worksop Manor, Buxton Hall and Tutbury Castle, as well as two London houses, a house in Chelsea and estates in Derbyshire, Yorkshire, Nottinghamshire, Shropshire and Staffordshire. Products from his iron- and lead-works were transported on his own ship, *The Talbot*. He was Lord Lieutenant of Derbyshire, Yorkshire and Nottinghamshire and immensely loyal to the Queen, who fondly addressed him as 'my good old man'.

Bess, anxious to build on her Derbyshire lands, could hardly have hoped for more. Their marriage was primarily a conjunction of assets, cemented by the intermarriages of four of their children. In 1568 Bess's daughter Mary was married to Shrewsbury's son by his first wife, Gilbert Talbot, and her son Henry to his daughter Grace (since the brides were only 12 and eight respectively, their husbands were packed off to Europe until such time as their wives could bear children). It was said that Bess made this marital package deal a condition of her acceptance of Shrewsbury. She certainly had the most to gain, in that she ensured her share of Shrewsbury's lands would remain within the family after her death. At a time when marriage among the nobility was designed to preserve and consolidate inheritance, such cold-blooded arrangements were common enough.

From the evidence of his portrait, Shrewsbury was dyspeptic, pinched and tremulous of appearance, with a high, narrow forehead, delicate, ascetic features, mournful eyes and a wispy beard. He was nervous, emotional, highly sensitive to perceived slights and burdened by responsibility. He was no match at all for the implacable will and cool head of his wife. Still, if his marriage was conceived as a business merger, familiarity bred affection – in the short term. In 1568 he wrote to Bess from Hampton Court, lamenting the fact that he'd heard nothing from her 'whyche drove me in dumpes', thanking his 'sweete none' (the odd endearment that they used for each other) for some 'podengs' and 'venyson' and adding, touchingly, 'As the pen writes so the heart thinks, that of all earthly joys that have happened to me, I thank God chiefest for you, for with you I have all joys and contentment of mind and without you death is more pleasant to me than life if I thought I should long be from you.' Another letter speaks of his 'faithful affection which I never tasted so deeply of before'.

Bess, seemingly an unlikely romantic object, had the gift for inspiring devotion. However, it was not a devotion she returned in kind. Many of her surviving letters to Shrewsbury are characterised by a peremptory tone not far removed from that which she used towards her steward. She wrote to him from Chatsworth, 'If you can not get my timber carried I must do without it though I greatly want it… I pray you let me know if I shall have the ton of iron, if you cannot spare it I must make shift to get it elsewhere… you promised to send me money before this time for me to buy oxen, but I see out of sight is out of mind with you… I will send you the bill of my wood stuff.' As a sweetener to these demands, the letter ends with a solicitous 'I have sent you lettuce for that you love them.' Elsewhere she complains about her lack of malt and hops, for brewing beer, and the poor quality of the 'sack' (wine) supplied by the Earl, one bottle so weak 'as though it were half water', and the other so old that it 'savours of the well'. 'You haste not to supply any want I have' was a familiar refrain from Bess, and, as Shrewsbury grew disenchanted with his role as purse and provider, affection turned to loathing.

In addition to funding Bess – no small matter – Shrewsbury had to provide for her children, for his own seven children, the eldest of whom, Francis, had large debts, and to maintain his numerous properties. If Shrewsbury's riches were great, so were his expenses, and in 1568 one more was added to the list: custodianship of Mary Queen of Scots, a task as psychologically testing as it was financially onerous.

At 26, Mary, nearly six feet tall, extremely attractive, famously charming, possessed of catastrophically bad judgement, addicted to intrigue, feared by the Queen and a rallying point for disaffected Catholics, was an unen-viable charge, especially for a nervous man with a demanding wife. Lord Burghley noted her ability 'by her great wit and sugared eloquence to win even such as before they shall come to her company shall have a great misliking'. Adroit deployment of feminine wiles had become Mary's principal strategy for survival during a life, shadowed, even by the standards of the age, by an unusually high quota of brutality and tragedy.

From the sophistication of the French Court, where she had been brought up as the betrothed and then the wife of Francis II, King of France, Mary had come, after her husband's death, to barbarian Scotland to take up her crown in 1561 (she was the granddaughter of James IV of Scotland and Margaret Tudor, Henry VIII's eldest sister, which also gave her a claim to the English throne). An unwise marriage in 1565 to the handsome degenerate, Lord Darnley, had foundered almost immediately. While pregnant she had witnessed the multiple stabbing – on the orders of her husband – of her Secretary, David Riccio. Shortly afterwards, Darnley himself had been found dead after an explosion at Kirk o' Field, in Edinburgh, for which Mary's new favourite, the Earl of Bothwell, was widely held responsible. Mary not only seemed reluctant to prosecute Bothwell, but then compounded her complicity by allowing her husband's murderer to abduct, ravish and, of necessity, marry her. The Scottish nobility rose in protest, Bothwell fled to Denmark, and Mary was forced to abdicate in favour of her young son, James VI. She was then imprisoned. In May 1568 she escaped and fled to England to throw herself on the not very tender mercies of her cousin Elizabeth.

The arrival of the kingdomless Mary put Elizabeth in a delicate position. On the one hand, she was anxious to be seen as a champion of the rights of a Queen, on the other, Mary was a Catholic with a claim to the English throne. In addition, her physical charms were said to eclipse

Elizabeth's own, though since the latter never granted her cousin an audience she was spared confirmation of such rumours. A mockery of a trial left Mary tainted by the suspicion of guilt of Darnley's murder without actually proving it. This suited Elizabeth: she was seen to observe the forms of justice without the penalties. Mary was to be detained in England, and it only remained to appoint a fitting custodian.

Shrewsbury qualified for this role on several counts: he was fanatically loyal to his Queen, he was a staunch Protestant, and he had a number of properties in the geographically secure Midlands. Also, in Bess, he had a wife whom the Queen regarded as equally trustworthy, indeed who was cast in a mould comparable to her own – both women were skilled manipulators, both possessed an indomitable will, with Bess inclining towards iron and Elizabeth towards caprice, and both declined to bow to male authority.

On Bess's marriage to the Earl, a friend reported the Queen as saying, 'I have been glad to see my Lady St Loe, but now more desirous to see my Lady Shrewsbury... there is no lady in this land that I better love and like.' Certainly in recent years Bess had been assiduously courting favour with carefully chosen New Year gifts. These were given to the Queen by her courtiers; money was acceptable, but imaginative effort was more appreciated. Knowing her Majesty's partiality for fine clothes, Bess presented her with a number of elaborately designed additions to her wardrobe: a skirt and doublet made of yellow satin, embroidered with silver and lined with black sarcenet; a dress of tawny satin decorated with lace of Venice gold and gold buttons. In the years to come Bess would show herself to be not quite the model subject, but in 1568 the Shrewsburys' star stood high.

With just a few weeks' notice they prepared Tutbury Castle in Derbyshire to receive their prisoner. Tapestries, bedding and carpets were provided from a store in the Tower, the Queen sent gold plate, and the remainder was supplied by Bess. Tutbury was rarely used by the Shrewsburys; it was damp, crumbling, extremely gloomy and hated by Mary, who wrote, 'I am in a walled enclosure, on the top of a hill, exposed to all the winds and inclemencies of heaven.' She reported that the furniture in her two 'miserable' little rooms became covered in mould in four days, that the privies gave off a 'continual stench', that she had a mere quarter of an acre of ground for exercise, 'a place, to look at, fitter to keep pigs in than to bear the name of garden', and that her health was suffering as a result of such deprivations. Mary's complaints about her health, most frequently of a pain in her side, were constant.

After conditions at Tutbury were acknowledged to be

unacceptable, she was moved to Wingfield, and later to Chatsworth, then back to Tutbury. In the course of 16 years, while Mary's fate hung in the balance, Shrewsbury shunted his prisoner between his properties a total of 46 times. These decampments, requiring royal consent on every occasion, were partly necessitated by the need to clean and air houses, but also to allow local supplies of food and fuel to be replenished. And they were no easy matter, involving some 200 people. Besides Mary and her servants, who were officially limited to 30 men and women but were often nearer to 50, there were some 40 soldiers, along with the supporters and hangers-on, most of them Scottish, who gravitated to her.

The expenses involved were considerable. In 1568 the Queen gave the Earl an allowance of £52 a week to cover Mary's care. In 1575 this was reduced to £30. Given the size of Mary's entourage and her insistence on certain standards of service and table – dinners with two courses of 16 dishes each, fine wines from France – it was a quite inadequate sum, less than half of what was required, and only intermittently dispensed. The Earl was permanently out of pocket and permanently aggrieved. After all, he had to maintain two households in one place – for himself and Bess, and for Mary – as well as separate establishments for his children because, for reasons of security, they were not supposed to be under the same roof as the Scottish Queen.

The Shrewsburys were as much prisoners of Mary as she of them and the demands of family were expected to take second place to those of state. When Bess's much-loved small grandson, two-year-old George Talbot, died, Shrewsbury had to request permission to be allowed to go to Chatsworth to comfort Bess, who had 'driven herself into such a case by her continual weeping as is like to breed in her further inconvenience'. Mary, of course, was dragged in his wake. It was ten years before the Earl was granted permission to leave his charge and come to Court. He was not allowed to visit his children. Such was the Queen's terror of Mary bewitching strangers that she was highly displeased to discover that Mary Talbot, Gilbert's wife, had given birth at Sheffield, where Mary was most frequently held. The Earl wrote to Lord Burghley in apology, assuring him that only the midwife had come to the house, and that he had christened the baby himself. He added that there had been an earthquake – 'God grant that it may be a warning to Mary.'

Mary seemingly needed some warning, since her appetite for intrigue appeared undimmed by captivity. Ciphers – coded messages – winged their way to and from her, hidden under stones in a visitor's hollowed-out staff or in the setting of a jewel. A plot for her escape, just one of many, was uncovered in 1570: she was to be smuggled out of a window at Chatsworth and taken to the Isle of Man. Damagingly for the Earl, a disaffected former servant who had left his service because he 'did mislike my Lord's marriage with his wife as divers of his friends did' (suggesting that Bess, who no doubt made her presence felt, was unpopular among the Earl's household) was revealed to be one of the plotters. But Mary's masterplan in the early years of her captivity was to marry the Duke of Norfolk (the existence of her third husband, Bothwell, who had lost his wits and was languishing in a Danish jail, was grandly overlooked). Norfolk was vain enough to be carried along by this ill-starred notion. When the Queen got wind of it he found himself in the Tower, an apparently insufficient deterrent because on his release he once again involved himself in Mary's intrigues and, more seriously, was found to be implicated in the Ridolfi plot, under which Philip of Spain was to invade England, depose Elizabeth and put Mary on the throne. For such treasonable activities Norfolk was executed, in 1572, and the Earl received orders that Mary be 'kept very straightly'. It would not be long, however, before she was plotting again.

The Earl found himself between a rock and a hard place. On the one hand there was Elizabeth with her stinginess, her suspicions, her paranoia about Mary, her insistence that while her cousin be treated with the respect her rank required, she be kept in conditions of the strictest restraint. On the other hand there was Mary with her constant complaints and demands – that she be allowed to go hunting or to ride in her coach or to take the waters at Buxton. To please both Queens required immense vigilance and diplomacy. It was a task the Earl felt increasingly unequal to. During these years he kept up a barrage of letters to Lord Burghley and to Elizabeth asking for the payment of Mary's allowance, justifying his conduct, complaining of the gout that crippled him, defending his honour. The latter, which Shrewsbury was said to 'esteemeth above all things', was of the utmost importance, the benchmark by which he defined himself. Having taken on the burden and expense of guarding Mary, he deemed his honour dented when Elizabeth begrudged him Mary's allowance and questioned his treatment of his prisoner. Later that precious honour would suffer further at the hands of his wife.

As to what Bess felt about being married to a man bound to the beguilingly tragic Queen of Scots, let alone about Mary herself, we can only guess. As the only woman, apart from her ladies-in-waiting, allowed access to Mary, there must have been a relationship of sorts. In the early days it was apparently amicable, so much so that Elizabeth's suspicions were raised and required a good deal of mollifying on the part of the Earl. He reported to Burghley that Mary 'daily resorts to my wife's chamber', where they would sit 'devising works' (embroidering, some of the results of which can be seen at Hardwick today), going on to assure him that their conversation was 'altogether of indifferent trifling matters'. But Mary and Bess were two wildly divergent personalities. When Robert Beale, a courtier, was sent by the Queen to report on the prisoner, he found her lying in the dark, weeping and claiming she was dying. Bess's verdict was tart, 'in her opinion she had known her far worse than she presently was'. Bess, in similar circumstances, would never have given way to wailing and hypochondria, but then of course Bess, the model of cautious calculation, would never have found herself in such circumstances. Mary's constant presence, her demands, the feminine charm she could not but exercise on every man in her orbit and which Shrewsbury had little enough of from his wife, must all have been irksome to Bess. Mary was the third person in a marriage that had scarcely had a chance to find its feet. The days of gossiping over the embroidery were short-lived. Whatever degree of goodwill had existed between the two women ultimately gave way to jealousy and recrimination, and soured, in the short term, thanks to Bess's designs on the English throne.

By 1574 Bess had one remaining unmarried daughter, 19-year-old Elizabeth Cavendish (her eldest daughter, Frances, had married Sir Henry Pierrepont, and her youngest, Mary, Gilbert Talbot, Bess's stepson). Almost nothing is known of Elizabeth, but she appears to have been of mild disposition, willing to fall in with her mother's wishes. Bess had been casting about for a suitable husband, but Shrewsbury had been digging his heels in about stumping up a dowry, and although she eventually 'by brawling did get three thousand pounds' various suitors fell by the wayside. 'There is few noblemens' sons in England that she hath not prayed for me to deal for at one time or other,' wrote Shrewsbury wearily. One such was Peregrine Bertie, the son of the Duchess of Suffolk (the Duchess, formerly married to Charles Brandon, Duke of Suffolk, was now the wife of her Master of the Horse, Richard Bertie, but was clearly reluctant to relinquish her title for the prosaic 'Mrs Bertie'). In the summer of 1574 the Duchess visited Bess at Chatsworth, possibly to discuss the Bertie match, but more probably to act as a go-between between Bess and Margaret, Countess of Lennox. For Bess had her eye on a new candidate for Elizabeth, of superior dynastic credentials: the Countess of Lennox's son, Charles Stuart.

Margaret, Countess of Lennox, the daughter of Henry VIII's eldest sister, Margaret Tudor, had suffered the agony of seeing six of her children die in infancy and one, Darnley, the erstwhile husband of Mary Queen of Scots, murdered. Her only surviving child was Charles Stuart, by all accounts a poor and sickly specimen, described even by his mother as 'my greatest dolour'. That summer of 1574 the elderly Countess asked for royal permission to leave Court in order to visit her Yorkshire estates. It was granted on the condition that she did not visit her former daughter-in-law, Mary Queen of Scots, or indeed go within 30 miles of her (it might be supposed that the Countess would hardly be inclined to pay a social call on Mary, tainted as she was with the guilt of Darnley's murder). In October she and Charles Stuart left London. Their first night was spent with the Duchess of Suffolk, in Northampton; their second, in Newark, Nottinghamshire. Here the Countess received a message from Bess, inviting the party to Rufford Abbey, a Shrewsbury property conveniently close by in Sherwood Forest, where Bess had positioned herself with Elizabeth. At Rufford the Countess fell ill and took to her bed for five days, while Charles and Elizabeth, obligingly bowing to maternal will and perhaps to the romance of their surroundings, fell in love. Before objections could be raised or minds changed, the young couple found themselves married.

The whole affair was either extremely fortuitous or carefully stage-managed. Since Bess was not a woman who believed in leaving things to chance, the latter seems most probable. But it was presented as a *coup de foudre*.

According to Shrewsbury, 'The young man is so far in love that belike he is sick without her.' The Earl, significantly, had not been consulted by Bess and news of the match sent him into a spin of alarm. To limit the damage, he dashed off letters playing down the responsibility of Bess and the Countess and denying any involvement of his own, 'I must confess to your Majesty as it was dealt in suddenly and without my knowledge.' No doubt harder words were used between husband and wife.

It was a marriage that the Queen, as Bess well knew, would not regard favourably. As long as Elizabeth remained childless, the next in the line of succession was Mary Queen of Scots, a Catholic and possibly a murderess. After Mary came her son, James VI of Scotland, and after James, Charles Stuart, Elizabeth Cavendish's young husband. A son from their marriage would have a strong claim to the throne and the Queen, ever sensitive on the subject of the succession, did not welcome the prospect of a new contender sprung on her from off-field. For her part in engineering the marriage, the Countess of Lennox found herself in the Tower for the third time, and all, as she said, for 'love matters'. What she hoped to gain from her son's match is unclear, since Elizabeth Cavendish brought neither noble blood nor fortune. It's a measure of both Bess's powers of persuasion and of the position she had carved for herself that her daughter was considered worthy of Charles Stuart at all. Bess, on the other hand, could contemplate the marvellous prospect of becoming grandmother to a king. Remarkably, she avoided the Tower, probably because her credit with the Queen stood high enough for a single breach of loyalty to be overlooked and, as the wife of Mary's jailor, she had made herself indispensable. Conscious of just how close to the wind she had sailed, Bess took particular pains with her New Year gift of 1575, consulting friends at Court and presenting the Queen with a gorgeous cloak of light-blue satin, trimmed with carnation velvet, a garment whose originality and cost, it was reported back to Bess, won the royal seal of approval.

In 1575, in the Lennox house in Hackney, Elizabeth Lennox gave birth to a girl, Arbella Stuart. By November the Countess of Lennox was out of the Tower and writing to Mary Queen of Scots, who appeared well-disposed to this new Stuart addition, to thank her for a gift sent to 'our little daughter'. A year later Charles Stuart died of consumption. Since there would be no male heir, Arbella became the focus of Bess's ambitions. Arbella, however, would prove intractable and in refusing, unlike her mother, to fall in with her grandmother's plans, presented a rare instance when Bess found her will thwarted. Such obduracy remained in the future: the young Arbella was the 'dearest jewel', fussed over, groomed and destined for, as Bess hoped, a glorious future.

Two years after Charles Stuart's death, the Countess of Lennox herself died, and, in 1582, Arbella's mother, Elizabeth, died also – a loss that Bess felt acutely, since, apart from the brief duration of her marriage, Elizabeth had been a more or less constant companion. Shrewsbury wrote that Bess 'so mourneth and lamenteth that she cannot think of aught but tears'. Arbella, the 'smale orphant', became dependent on Bess who, as her guardian, took up the battle for her rights, for the return of her inheritance. Charles Stuart's Scottish lands had been seized by James IV of Scotland and the Lennox title, the Earldom, given to the elderly Robert Stuart, the Bishop of Caithness. On the Countess's death the Queen, with characteristic high-handedness, took over her English estates, announcing that she needed the income to pay Margaret's funeral expenses. Arbella had been left her grandmother's jewels, but these were carried off to Scotland and ended up in the hands of James who, being partial to a jewel, had no intention of giving them up. Arbella was left with nothing but her royal blood.

In the autumn of 1578 Bess came to Court where the Earl of Leicester, a friend to both Shrewsburys – 'Next to her Majesty there are no two people in England better welcome than your Lord and yourself,' he wrote – arranged for Bess to have 'one great chamber with some

other little room' in his own quarters. This was recip-
rocated hospitality, as Leicester had enjoyed sojourns at
Chatsworth and Buxton. Some years earlier, Bess had
succeeded in persuading the Queen to make an annual
allowance of £200 for Arbella and £400 for her mother,
Elizabeth. After the latter's death, which she could not
'remember but with a sorrowful troubled mind', Bess
wrote to Lord Burghley, once again calling in the favours
of friendship, asking him to remind the Queen 'to confirm
that grant of the whole six hundred pounds yearly for the
education of my dearest jewel Arbella'. This education,
the 'dearest jewel' being of royal blood, as Bess pointed
out, was an expensive business. Her petition fell on deaf
ears and Elizabeth Lennox's £400 was withdrawn. Nevertheless Bess made sure Arbella was provided with lessons
in French, Italian, Spanish, Latin (a scrap of paper at
Chatsworth signed by William Cavendish and his 11-year-
old son promises the latter a rapier, a dagger, an embroidered girdle and a pair of spurs if he will speak Latin 'till
Lent Assizes next' with his cousin Arbella), Hebrew,
Greek, music and dancing. It was the kind of rigorous,
classical education enjoyed by only the most high-ranking
young women, and one that had certainly not been
available to Bess; an education, in fact, fit for a queen.

Bess's efforts to promote and secure Arbella's position
in the succession, were unflagging and in 1583 she was

scheming once again, this time to marry the eight-year-old Arbella to the four-year-old Robert Dudley. The prospective groom was the son of the Earl of Leicester by his second wife, Lettice Knollys. A marriage between Arbella and Robert would co-join royal blood on her part with powerful connections on his, and for those very reasons it would be unwelcome to the Queen, who was therefore kept in the dark. Leicester was enthusiastic, but negotiations came to nothing because little Robert died in 1584. It was the first of many failed attempts to find Arbella a suitable husband. Elizabeth was once again magnanimous towards Bess, but the proposed marriage fatally antagonised the Queen of Scots. Mary had shown herself willing to lend support to Arbella's claim to the Lennox inheritance – indeed she had made a will in 1577 bequeathing the Lennox title to Arbella, a document nobody took the slightest notice of – but Bess pushing her granddaughter towards the English throne, which Mary considered to be rightfully hers, was quite another matter. She wrote, furiously, 'Nothing has alienated the Countess of Shrewsbury from me more than the vain hope she has conceived of setting the Crown on her granddaughter Arbella's head by means of marrying her to the son of the Earl of Leicester.'

Mary was not the only person Bess had alienated. By 1583 the Shrewsburys were living apart. The atmosphere at Sheffield, where the Earl watched over Mary, had become poisonous – as Marmyon, a servant of Bess's, described in a letter to Sir Francis Willoughby, in which he begged for permission to enter his service, since 'this house is a hell' made by the 'broyle or kind of tragedy' that had developed between husband and wife. Bess had taken herself off to Chatsworth, an act of defiance that the Earl chose to regard as grounds for separation. He promptly cut off her annual allowance of £800. The custodianship of the Queen of Scots had strained the Earl beyond his limits. He was blaming Bess, and by extension Bess's servants, for making trouble between himself and Elizabeth I, and, in consequence, for a further reduction of his allowance for Mary's care. Such accusations, irrational and implausible though they sound, were typical of the random missiles he impotently hurled at his wife.

In decamping to the still unfinished Chatsworth, Bess was succumbing to the old lure of bricks and mortar. Back in 1577 the Earl had complained to his son, Gilbert Talbot, 'How often have I cursed the building at Chatsworth for want of her company.' Just as with William St Loe, all that was romantic and passionate in Bess was engaged not by her husband but by her building. A few years later Shrewsbury would write querulously to his wife, 'I pray you send me Accres as soon as you can for

I may spare him no longer.' This was Thomas Accres, the brilliant mason, whom Shrewsbury required for his own building project, the splendid Worksop. But squabbles over a mason were merely symptomatic of a deeper rift.

The Shrewsburys' quarrels began with trivialities – an incident where Bess's embroiderers were locked out of Sheffield by a servant of Shrewsbury's – escalated into open warfare and became mired in pettiness. Bess reported that she had been publicly abused by her husband in front of the servants. On another occasion, the Earl arrived at the gates of Chatsworth with 40 men to find his entrance barred by William Cavendish, his stepson. For such 'insolent behaviour' William found himself in the Fleet jail. There were skirmishes between servants belonging to the Earl and those of Bess. After a programme of harassment, Bess left Chatsworth for Hardwick, where, to distract herself from her woes, and to provide a much-needed refuge, she started rebuilding the Old Hall. The Earl accused her of taking with her furnishings belonging to him. But behind such complaints were fundamental differences: here was a strong woman pursuing an agenda which did not encompass the weak man to whom she was married. Bess's schemes, her 'devices and designs' as Shrewsbury called them, to bring her family closer to the English throne, were conducted behind her husband's back since she knew full well he would be too much of an alarmist to countenance them. And there was the all-important question of money, the issue on which the Shrewsburys sharpened their knives and on which they would both prove absolutely intractable. In 1572 Shrewsbury had signed a deed of gift whereby he made over to William and Charles Cavendish the lands Bess had brought him on their marriage, with Bess retaining a life interest. In exchange he was let off paying 'great Somes of money' – rumoured to be £20,000 each – that the marriage settlement required him to make over to William and Charles on their coming of age, as well as paying Bess's debts. Much of the disagreement between the Shrewsburys hinged on the interpretation of this deed. The Earl claimed that the deed was made for the benefit of Bess, not of her sons; Bess alleged the Earl had been collecting rents from lands that belonged to her. The Earl justified this by claiming that Bess had been selling land without his consent, which was forbidden by the deed and thus rendered it void.

The minutiae of these disputes are bewildering, but they are animated by Shrewbury's unshakeable belief that Bess and her children were united in a conspiracy to bleed him dry. 'I have done many good things for my wife and her children and they have requited me evil in doing and procuring that might most hurt and trouble me,' he wrote. Unreasonable in many respects, he was not unreasonable in this, for Bess and her family had benefited enormously from their relationship to Shrewsbury.

He wrote to Lord Burghley, 'Till Francis Talbot's death she and her children sought of my favour, but since those times they have sought for themselves and never for me.' Francis Talbot, Shrewsbury's debt-ridden eldest son, had perished in the plague in 1582. His death meant that Gilbert Talbot, married to Bess's daughter Mary, was now heir and Gilbert, whose relations with his stepmother were good, ranged himself on the side of Bess. This was an added bitterness for the Earl, who wrote of the 'crafty devices' on the part of Bess, her sons and Gilbert 'to maintain and strengthen their confederacy against me'. He did his best to stop Gilbert from seeing Bess, but he could hardly keep Mary Talbot from her mother. He claimed that he had no wish for Gilbert to hate his wife 'tho I doo deteste her mother', but in the next breath he admitted he thought them both as bad as each other or, as he more poetically put it, 'I think nethar barrell bettar herring of them bothe.' He refused to pay Gilbert's debts on the grounds that he ought to be able to live perfectly well on his allowance if Mary would consent to lessen her 'pomp and courtlike manner'.

The Earl, with his own debts as well as those of his children, Bess's demands and the costs of keeping Mary Queen of Scots, was feeling the pinch. 'My riches they talk of are in other men's purses,' he wrote pathetically.

Meanwhile Bess had been quietly and consistently buying land in and around Derbyshire in the names of William and Charles Cavendish (this was her usual policy; it meant that Shrewsbury could not get his hands on the property and she kept a life interest). The sums of money involved were considerable. In 1583 she spent £9,500 on buying Hardwick from her brother, in William's name. By 1584 she had invested £24,700 in land. A proportion of this money must have somehow been extracted from the Earl. Bess's accounts record regular payments to William whom she had made her second-in-command, presumably for buying land or other purchases, and William made regular trips to London where he took and returned with bags of money. In none of these shadowy transactions was the Earl consulted or included. Bess was no longer showing her hand.

Then into the fray stepped Mary Queen of Scots. There was no love lost between Mary and Bess since the latter's impudent machinations, as Mary viewed them, on behalf of her granddaughter Arbella. It was inevitable that she would attempt to exploit the dissension between the Shrewsburys. On Bess's part it would seem entirely natural that she should have grown to resent Mary. The beleaguered Earl himself wrote of his charge's 'alluring grace', 'pretty Scottish accent' and 'searching wit clouded with mildness'. Bess was believed to be jealous which, given the absence of passionate feeling for her husband, seems unlikely. But she very possibly encouraged such a belief in the interests of making trouble for the Earl, who reported Bess as saying that 'the Scottish Queen could rule me in all things against her'. In 1584 a rumour began to circulate that the Earl and Mary had had an affair and a child, or even two, together. Both parties were outraged and Mary loudly attributed the rumour to Bess and her sons. It was hotly denied. Mary, when not engaged in plots to marry Philip of Spain, busied herself, by her own admission, in making trouble for Bess. She wrote of her intention to 'implicate indirectly the Countess of Shrewsbury' in the spreading of the rumours. She claimed that Bess's servants and Bess herself had brought her 'ciphers', that Bess had promised she would help her escape, that Bess could be 'gained by me whenever I pleased with a bribe of 2,000 crowns' (allegations which seem highly improbable, given Bess's caution and lack of sympathy for Mary).

For good measure Mary composed a letter in early 1584, later known as the 'scandal letter', addressed to the Queen. In this she reported that Bess had regaled her with tales of Elizabeth as an insatiable and physically deformed nymphomaniac, numbering the Earl of Leicester and Sir Christopher Hatton among her lovers. She described Bess as having ridiculed the Queen for her susceptibility to flattery 'such as that none dared to look you full in the face because it shone like the sun and when on her last visit to Court, she and the late Countess of Lennox dare not look at each other when addressing you, for fear of bursting into roars of laughter'. If nothing else, the last vignette of Bess and her daughter trying to keep straight faces in the royal presence has the ring of authenticity. Mary's letter was almost certainly never sent, but it gives a measure of her loathing for Bess as well as Bess's capacity for mischief. In the summer of 1584 the alleged affair between Mary and the Earl became the subject of an inquiry. Bess and her sons, William and Charles, swore the rumour was a 'false and malicious invention' and denied all responsibility. Their denial was accepted. So, too, was Shrewsbury's resignation as Mary's jailor.

Two leitmotifs run through the breakdown of the Shrewsburys' marriage: his venom and her forbearance. The Earl was a man whose emotional responses frequently appeared disproportionate to their causes. Bess, once his 'only joy', metamorphosed into a devil. As Gilbert Talbot put it, 'All his wonted love and affection is clean turned to the contrary.' Bess, his father told Gilbert, 'scolded like one from the Bank'; she called him 'knave, foole and beast to his face and hathe mocked and mowed at him with words and gestures'. He wrote of 'her wicked dealings sticking so deeply in my heart as albeit for charity's sake I may forgive, yet I am never to forget them'. He alleged that Bess had threatened him and attempted to 'dishonour' him with 'slandrous speeches and sinister practices'. He asked, tellingly, that he be allowed 'that defence of my honour that I may be reckoned the husband and not the wife'. This was central to the Earl's resentment, the sense that he'd been emasculated by Bess. Over and over in his letters to Leicester or Burghley or the Queen herself, written in a crabbed, illegible hand, he returns to his 'honour', so undermined by the wife who has 'ruled and overruled' him. There is something of Shakespeare's Lear about Shrewsbury, in the violence of his language, in his uncontrolled, impotent rage, his self-pity, his blind resistance to reason. 'How sharper than a serpent's tooth it is/To have a thankless child!' Substitute 'wife' for 'child' and you could have Shrewsbury railing at Bess. He wrote to her, 'There cannot be any wife more forgetful of her duty and less careful to please her husband than you have been... I have seen thoroughly into all your devices and designs, your insatiable and greedy appetite did betray you, your own living at my hands could not content you, nor yet a great part of mine... your fair words are no bait for me... though they appear beautiful yet are they mixed with a hidden poison.'

But where in this maelstrom of bitterness and accusation did Bess stand? Was she the devil Shrewsbury believed her to be? Malice, too impractical an impulse, its effects too uncertain, was not part of her make-up. Bess was a strategist; her schemes framed by the long view which did not allow for small-minded vengefulness. If she can be cleared of malice, however, she was not perhaps so innocent of disingenuousness. Her public stance in the face of her husband's charges was clear enough – the bewildered distress of the wronged wife. It was a policy that could only reflect well on her. She wrote to the Earl, 'I will leave no way unsought to attain your favour… my heart, notwithstanding what I have suffered, thirsteth after your prosperity and desires nothing so much as to have your love… I know my Lord that hatred must grow of something and how I have deserved your indignation is invisible to me.'

Where the Earl was wildly abusive and irrational, Bess was unfailingly placatory and reasonable. She proclaimed that her sole desire was for reconciliation, though such a desire could be safely professed in the knowledge that Shrewsbury was too far entrenched in his opposition for it to be realised. Her letters could be used against her and Bess was above all things careful. She was also aware that to be publicly estranged from one's husband, in the sexually puritanical atmosphere fostered by the Queen, was a scandalous state. Elizabeth, as Bess knew only too well, took a dim view of squabbling couples. Bess required a nominal husband; the umbrella of Shrewsbury's wealth and position within which to operate. But she miscalculated with Shrewsbury, who was undoubtedly tinged with paranoia, exacerbated by nervous strain and gout. She certainly had no need for a husband hurling insults, appropriating monies and property she believed to be hers and interfering with the course of her business. When it came to financial considerations, Bess was markedly less conciliatory.

The collapse of the Shrewsburys' marriage in the early 1580s was treated as a matter of national importance and much discussed and commented upon. 'The warres contynue betwixt the Erl of Shrewsberie and the Contes', reads a typical letter of the time, 'the Contes is humble in speech and stowte in actions' (an apt summing up of Bess's conduct). The Queen wrote to Shrewsbury with the sympathetic concern of a kindly aunt, anxious that his marital disputes 'have greatly disquieted you, whose years require repose' and adding, 'We have long desired for your own good and quiet, that all matters of difference between the Countess your wife, her sons and you might be brought to some good composition.' There is steel behind that 'we'. The phrasing is gentle; the message crystal clear. In 1584 a commission of enquiry was set up to arbitrate between the warring couple. The gist of its ruling was simple enough: Bess was to keep her lands and the Earl was to keep Bess. The Earl was to give back £2,000 that he'd appropriated in rents from his wife's lands; Bess was to pay her husband an annual £500; William and Charles Cavendish were to keep lands bought over the last 12 years. Bess had the satisfaction of seeing herself vindicated and no doubt congratulated herself on her policy of patient reason and injured virtue. For the Earl it was a very bitter pill, an insult to his loyalty to his Queen. He wrote that he would abide by the order 'though no curse or plague in the earth could be more grievous'. In fact he did no such thing and ignored the order.

His wife lost no time in writing to Sir Francis Walsingham (Elizabeth's Principal Secretary of State). It is often tempting to see Bess as a kind of automaton, unwavering and, if not exactly inhuman, impervious to the frailties and vulnerabilities that make for humanity. The firm, sloping strokes of her pen betray little of weariness or doubt. But here she lets herself appear as a woman bowed and crushed by her sufferings. She begs for her Majesty's protection. She asks that her sons be allowed to 'seek their livings in some other place and that only their deer may be provided'; she hopes that their 'banishment' will 'pacify his [Shrewsbury's] indignation', and she concludes, poignantly, 'For my self I shall find some friend for meat and drink and so end my life.' She signs herself 'your distressed desolate friend'. Either Bess, worn down by the Earl's relentless hostility, was faltering or this was a calculated bid for sympathy. Probably it was a little of both. At any rate Bess, now 60, showed no signs of embracing obscurity and death, and the letter had the desired effect.

A second inquiry held at Ashford in Derbyshire reiterated the ruling of the first, binding the Earl by the vast sum of £40,000 to reconcile himself with his wife. He was to take Bess back under his roof. She was to return to him the household items removed from Chatsworth. Again the Earl proved intractable and Bess was soon complaining that only £850 of the £2,000 had been repaid, that her tenants were being displaced and that suits were being brought against her. She asked for 'speedy redress'. The Earl submitted a list of the articles taken from Chatsworth: plate, sheets, jewels, feather beds, hangings, New Year gifts. Bess briskly deleted every item on the list, with tart comments – the sheets were worn out, the plate had been sold, the remainder were dismissed as 'things of small value and mere trifles for so great and rich a nobleman to bestow on his wife in 19 years'. Nineteen years of marriage stood shipwrecked on the bed sheets. Recovering her patience, Bess wrote to her husband, regretting that the 'denial of the plate' should stand in the way of reconciliation, insisting that she desired 'no more than her Majesty's order gives'. She could not, though, resist needling him with reminders of expenditure on her behalf that he seems to have forgotten: 'I marvel you call not to mind this, when so small things be recited, as £500 allowed in money yearly, hides and fells which you paid me £100 for and £80 which was servants wages.' But she still wishes herself 'without offence with you'. A further order from the Queen and a private interview between herself and the Earl brought partial results. Bess moved into Wingfield.

While the Shrewsburys' quarrels rumbled on, the final act of the tragedy of Mary Queen of Scots was played out. The discovery of the Babington Plot, by which Elizabeth was to be assassinated and Mary placed on the throne, sounded her death knell. At her trial, which Shrewsbury attended, evidence was produced that proved that Mary, at the very least, had condoned the plot. Anthony Babington and his fellow conspirators endured the lingering agony of being hung, castrated and disembowelled, a spectacle which was apparently too much for even hardened Elizabethans. On 8 February 1587 Mary was executed. It was Shrewsbury's grisly duty in his capacity as Earl Marshal to give the nod to the executioner. It took three blows of the axe to sever her head. The Earl whose charge Mary had been for 16 years, who could not have been immune to her charm and who was forced to witness the dignity with which she met her death, stood by and wept.

The peace between the Shrewsburys was brief. Bess wrote to Burghley from Wingfield, claiming that, if it were not for Burghley's support, 'grefe and dyspleasur would have enddyd my dayes'. She informed him that the Earl had now made conditions intolerable by withholding basic provisions – beef, mutton and corn – as well as fuel. He was effectively starving her out. 'What he will do further I know not,' wrote Bess. What the Earl did was to take himself off to a property at Sheffield, Handsworth Manor, and into the arms of his housekeeper, a Mrs Eleanor Britton (the unfortunate Shrewsbury was clearly a magnet for rapacious women, since after his death Mrs Britton snatched quantities of money and jewels from under the noses of his heirs). His loathing for Bess remained undimmed. William Overton, the Bishop of Coventry and Lichfield, wrote offering some marriage guidance: 'If shrewdness or sharpness may be just cause for separation betwixt man and wife I think few men in England would keep their wives long, for it is a common jest yet true in some sense that there is one shrew in all the world and every man has her and I doubt not that your great wisdom and experience have taught you to bear with a woman as a weak vessel.' Presumably he refrained from allusions to 'weak vessels' when he applied to Bess for a loan of £100 a few years later.

In November 1590 the Earl of Shrewsbury, 62 years old and crippled and twisted with gout and bitterness, died. His death was not greatly mourned by Bess. It brought an end to years of hostility and left her free to pour her energies into the building of her beloved Hardwick.

The fact that Hardwick Old Hall, still unfinished, stood a mere 100 yards distant did not deter Bess in the slightest. The large and splendid but architecturally mismatched Old Hall belonged to the beleaguered years of estrangement from Shrewsbury; the New was born out of a triumphant widowhood. It saw Bess drawing on her building expertise, indulging her whims and, armed with Robert Smythson's 'platt', erecting a house that would inspire envy and awe.

***

The inscription on Smythson's tomb describes him as 'architector and surveyor unto the most worthy house of Wollaton and divers others of great account'. An 'architector' in 16th-century England meant little more than a craftsman of lowly social status, albeit highly skilled, who could produce basic designs. Sometimes he was simply a supervisor of works. After training as a stonemason Smythson had worked on Longleat for 12 years, and also on Wardour Castle. From 1580 he had been involved in the design and building of the monumental Wollaton Hall, Sir Francis Willoughby's Nottinghamshire house. He remained at Wollaton, employed in a general capacity, until his death in 1614 but, when not engaged in collecting rents or drawing up inventories of bedding for Sir Francis, he also found time to remodel Worksop Manor for the Earl of Shrewsbury and to draw up his 'platt' for Hardwick. If Smythson brought architectural coherence – so lacking in the Old Hall – to Hardwick, his involvement went no further than the plan. As of all Elizabethan houses, the building became a collaboration between the patron, Bess, and her craftsmen.

The building accounts for Hardwick, kept by Henry Jenkinson, who also served as Bess's household priest, reveal the mechanics of 16th-century construction and the skeleton of an emerging house. By the autumn of 1591 the walls of the ground floor were complete and a contract had been signed with John and Christopher Rhodes, a fraternal team of masons who had worked at Wollaton, to quarry and cut the stone for the remainder of the house. Blocks of sandstone, known as ashlar, were placed on beds of mortar mixed with oyster shells (oysters appeared regularly on Bess's table) over a core of infill, with another skin of ashlar inside. The mortar was made from limestone, burned in kilns alongside the house; ash from the kilns was mixed with water and laid on hay to make flooring for the interiors. Materials were used with maximum efficiency.

The fact that Bess was able to rely on her resource-rich Derbyshire lands to supply these materials explains the surprisingly low building costs. According to the accounts (admittedly incomplete), the Old and New Hardwicks were built for £5,500, which seems a negligible sum given that Bess had spent £9,500 on buying the original house and lands. Sandstone came from a quarry just below the house; blackstone and alabaster for the monumental fireplaces came from Ashford and Tutbury respectively; limestone came from Skegby and Crich; and timber from woods at Teversall, Penrich and Heath – all owned by Bess and all within a 20-mile radius of Hardwick. These were hauled in carts by oxen or carried on packhorses. At Wingfield, a Shrewsbury property, Bess had an ironworks under the supervision of a Sylvester Smith, as well as a glassworks.

The latter meant a substantial saving. Glass manufacture had already been vastly improved by the skills of French glassmakers, imported into Sussex in the 1560s, but it remained extremely costly. Bess paid her glazier Richard Snidall £290, proportionately a very large sum, for the cutting and setting of the glass for Hardwick. So her chief outlay was labour and labour was cheap.

Key to the success of building houses such as Hardwick

were experienced, reliable craftsmen, like the Rhodes brothers; they were treated well and they rewarded Bess with their loyalty. Skilled workers had contracts or were paid at piece-rates (in lump sums, according to the task), while the most valued of all, such as Thomas Accres and Abraham Smith, were permanently on the payroll and remained so until Bess's death. Smith, the creator of the extraordinary plaster frieze in the high great chamber, and Accres, who was responsible for many of Hardwick's marble and alabaster overmantels, both had rent-free farms and were paid a half-yearly wage of £6 13s 4d.

Labourers were paid by the day, an average of 6d, which was slightly less than the norm, but Bess laid on basic food – butter, milk, pease, oatmeal and herrings. She did not provide accommodation. As the house went up, its builders probably slept within its walls. Masons enjoyed the privilege of 'lodges', which were lean-tos, put up against the walls, in which to work; the plumber had a 'plumery'. Women were occasionally used for lighter tasks – polishing stone, carrying water to the men, mixing plaster, collecting rubbish – at the cheaper rate of 1d a day.

Hardwick required furnishing, and in October 1951, putting a halt to the building which largely stopped anyway during the winter months, Bess, accompanied by her 16-year-old granddaughter Arbella Stuart, decamped to London for an eight-month shopping spree. She travelled in considerable style. A coach (recently introduced into England and, despite being unsprung, a coveted accessory) pulled by six horses whose harness buckles were cast in shining ES's, rocked and rumbled its way southwards, carrying Bess, Arbella and their ladies-in-waiting. The rest of the party, William and Charles Cavendish and assorted servants, about 40 in all, followed on horseback. Running footmen wearing the light-blue livery of the Cavendishes alerted approaching towns so church bells could be rung in welcome. Alms were distributed to the poor and crowds lined the streets. It was a spectacle with all the hallmarks of a royal progress. After a seven-day journey over pothole-ridden roads, Bess and her entourage established themselves in Shrewsbury House in Chelsea (where Cheyne Walk is today), which had undergone an anticipatory programme of alteration and refurbishment. Furniture had been brought from Derbyshire and 40 sheep and two oxen – a walking larder – driven up from Bess's Leicestershire estate. Chelsea in 1591 was little more than a village surrounded by fields, but the river provided easy transport to the royal palaces, at Whitehall, Richmond and Greenwich, and to the City.

Apart from fitting out Hardwick, there were other reasons for Bess's London visit. The Earl of Shrewsbury's death had turned Gilbert Talbot from friend to foe; the father's grievances had become those of the son. The Earl had left debts, and the extravagant, quarrelsome Gilbert had large debts of his own. He was prevaricating over paying Bess's settlement under the Earl's will and claiming that Bess was appropriating land that wasn't hers. Gilbert's behaviour, complained Bess pithily, 'doth stick sore in her teeth'. There was to be a legal case to settle their differences. To ensure that this was heard in Derbyshire, where Bess could be confident of the outcome, influential London lawyers had to be courted and cajoled.

There was also the matter of a husband for Arbella. Arbella had spent her childhood being shunted between Bess and her aunts and uncles and with Gilbert and Mary Talbot in particular. A less personally alluring figure than her aunt by marriage, Mary Queen of Scots, Arbella nevertheless shared with the former the Stuart charm and the Stuart recklessness. She was already showing signs of wilfulness. Her last visit to Court three years earlier had ended in disgrace after an incident in which her much-vaunted royal blood had apparently gone to her head and she had tried, it was reported, to 'claim first place' over the other ladies present on going into chapel. For such unseemly airs, the Queen, who may also have taken exception to Arbella's supposed flirtation with the new royal favourite, the Earl of Essex, had 'ordered her back to her private existence'. She had since been forgiven and

Bess was on the lookout for a husband who would consolidate her claim to the throne.

Bess and Arbella's first important social engagement was to attend Court for the Twelve Days of Christmas, a whirl of plays, masques, feasting, dancing and bear-baiting. This required some essential shopping. Bess's December accounts record the purchase of 50 yards of damask, 50 yards of velvet, 40 yards of satin, quantities of black taffeta and black Spanish lace (these would have been for Bess, the sober widow) and blue and white starches for lace collars and ruffs (starch-making techniques, using wheat, had been introduced into England by a Dutch woman in the 1560s). Twenty one pounds was spent on a pair of bracelets 'set with diamonds, pearls and rubies', 14 shillings 'a piece' on 'five little jewels' and 6s 4d on 'another little one of a bee'. The Court was at Whitehall for Christmas, the largest of the Tudor palaces, a sprawling conglomeration of 2,000 rooms covering 23 acres and decorated in medieval style with Holbein's great portraits of Henrys VII and VIII and their Queens looming from the walls of the Privy Chamber. Whitehall catered admirably to Elizabethan taste for colour and spectacle, with a tennis court, a tiltyard, a cockpit and gardens enlivened by 34 heraldic beasts mounted on brightly painted pillars, along with a sundial that told the time in 30 different ways and a multi-jetted fountain.

Back in Shrewsbury House Bess received visitors, made contact with influential Court figures and set about out-manoeuvring Gilbert Talbot. Old friends, fellow widows, such as Lady Cheek, Lady Cobham and Lady Bacon, the mother of Sir Francis, came to gossip and to borrow money. Courtiers such as the Admiral of the Fleet, Lord Howard, and the Lord High Treasurer, Lord Buckhurst, came to pay their respects. To defeat Gilbert, Bess needed powerful allies. Sir William Cordell, the Master of the Rolls, who had already been warmed up with presents, was invited to dinner. Her tactics paid off and a sub-stantial £430 in legal charges brought the desired result: the case would be heard in Derbyshire.

In the meantime there was more shopping to be done. The shops of London in the 1590s were concentrated along Cheapside. Here Bess, picking her way through stinking, unpaved streets, would have found goldsmiths, pewterers, tailors, cordwainers, glovers, drapers and haberdashers. She spent more than £300 on refurbishing her own and Arbella's wardrobes, on perfumed gloves and shoes of Spanish leather (for Court visits), on velvet shoes and 'pantables' (overshoes), a dress trimmed with red baize and a powdered ermine gown. She bought a luxurious litter for herself, gorgeously upholstered in tawny velvet, with a silk fringe and windows of tawny and gold parchment. For Hardwick she acquired vast quantities, over £1,200-worth, of gold and silver plate, as well as standing cups, basins, looking glasses, candlesticks and hangings. From Sir William Hatton she bought three sets of tapestries, including the Gideon tapestries at £326, for the long gallery, with £5 deducted, at her insistence, to cover the cost of changing the Hatton arms to her own.

In May she and Arbella hired three boats and journeyed down the river to join the Court, this time at Greenwich. A match between Arbella and Rainutio Farnese, the son of the Duke of Parma, was under discussion. There were political as well as dynastic benefits for the Queen and for Bess in such a union. The Duke of Parma commanded the Spanish forces fighting the English in the Spanish Netherlands; he could also claim descent from John of Gaunt. Elizabeth was anxious for peace and Bess for a suitably well-connected husband. In order that Rainutio could look over his prospective bride, Nicholas Hilliard was commissioned to paint a miniature – the 16th-century equivalent of a Polaroid – of Arbella. On 27 July Bess paid Mr Hilliard 40 shillings for the portrait. But negotiations came to nothing because the Duke of Parma, who had been his son's chief attraction, died, and with him hopes of an end to the war with Spain. Arbella remained husbandless but, having reintroduced her at Court and into the Queen's good graces, Bess remained optimistic. Altogether her sojourn in London could be counted a triumph: Gilbert had been out-smarted, her lands had been secured, Hardwick would look resplendent. Leaving Arbella at Court, Bess, carried in her new litter, began her journey home. Behind her came one waggon piled with plate and nine more stacked with loot. She had spent a total of £6,360.

En route to Derbyshire, Bess made a detour to inspect Sir Christopher Hatton's Holdenby in Northamptonshire and Sir Francis Willoughby's Wollaton near Nottingham. She was assessing the competition and in search of ideas. A housekeeper showed her around the vast and empty Holdenby, which was to deteriorate almost as fast as the career of its builder (a man described by a contemporary as 'a mere vegetable of the Court that sprung up at night and sank again at his noon'). At heavily magnificent Wollaton, Bess would have envied the glorious prospect room, if not the fortunes of Sir Francis. The Willoughbys, like the Hardwicks, were provincial gentry, who had risen in the ranks thanks to royal favour and lucrative deposits of coal. The profits from the latter were poured into the building of Wollaton. Sir Francis, with his own architectural library, was an unusually cultured patron but, unlike Bess, an extremely poor businessman, and disastrous investments and overly grandiose projects had left him with large debts. He was in need of a loan. Bess agreed to lend him £3,000, with annual interest of

£300, on the security of five manors (worth about £15,000). The mortgage was put in Arbella's name and since the loan was never repaid the properties ultimately became hers. A relatively modest outlay produced substantial returns. It was the kind of canny transaction in which Bess specialised.

Bess was back at Hardwick by August 1592. She found that John and Christopher Rhodes had cut stone, at 4d a foot, for 41 first-floor windows and that the scaffolding for the walls of the first floor was in place. A key figure in the building of Hardwick, and especially during the periods when Bess was away, was John Balechouse, otherwise known as John 'Painter' because no one could pronounce his Flemish name. Balechouse was a painter responsible for the frieze in the long gallery, but he was also trusted to oversee operations. He was paid an annual £2, and granted a farm at Ault Hucknall and the occasional random cash reward – '£10 Geven to John Paynter of my goodwill' – which Bess, an exacting but essentially benevolent employer, clearly believed in as a means of keeping her workforce sweet. On another occasion, Thomas Accres was given 10 shillings for inventing an 'engine', a kind of sawmill, for cutting blackstone, with which Bess must have been especially delighted since her munificence extended to his wife who received 20 shillings 'to buy her a gowne'. Conversely, unsatisfactory workers could expect short shrift. Every two weeks Bess ran a gimlet eye over the accounts. 'Because the walls ryse and be not well nor all of one collor therfor they most be perfectly wheyted at the plasterer's charge,' she wrote.

During the autumn of 1592 those walls rose as far as the second floor. Hardwick was emerging at surprising speed. In April 1593 Bess signed a contract with her carpenters, Peter and William Yates, to make the roof for £50. This was of lead supported by 16 vast timber trusses which would have been heaved and manoeuvred into place using nothing more sophisticated than ropes. 'Payd to John Roods the 5th May for hewing two windows contayning in measure one hundred 13 foots apece at 4half d the foot and so he is payd for 40 windowes for the 3 storye'. By October 1593, the 40 windows for the top floor had been set.

With the shell of Hardwick in place and final touches still being made to the Old Hall where Bess was living, she took on a third project, a house a few miles distant called Oldcotes. It was to be a smaller and less ambitious version of Hardwick and was intended for her son, William, who needed an establishment of his own. William, Bess's second son, was her most satisfactory child, the safe pair of hands required to preserve and build on what she had begun. He was stolid, reliable and efficient, with all his mother's instincts for acquisition, but none of her flair (though he did have the imagination to employ the philosopher Thomas Hobbes as tutor to his son; Hobbes occupied one of the turret rooms at Hardwick). But those qualities that endeared him to Bess, made him unpopular elsewhere and he had a reputation for miserliness. William's younger brother, Charles, was an altogether more dashing figure, a brilliant rider and swordsman, a lover of music and a lifelong friend, regardless of their parents' quarrels, to Gilbert Talbot.

But the most interesting and attractive-sounding of Bess's sons was her eldest, 'my bad son Henry'. Henry had a large number of illegitimate children (though none by his marriage to Grace Talbot) for which he was known as 'the common bull to all Derbyshire and Staffordshire'. He was as promiscuous with money as he was with his favours. He loved a lost cause – he had got into trouble for smuggling letters for Mary Queen of Scots – and he relished any opportunity to thwart his mother. In 1589 he made a romantic if gruelling journey by ship and waggon to Constantinople, possibly undertaken on Bess's behalf to investigate the potential for trade. The Turkish carpets at Hardwick are probably souvenirs from this expedition. But Henry, as far as Bess was concerned, was quite unfit to head the next generation of Cavendishes. She could not prevent him from inheriting Chatsworth, but she ensured that no further benefits came his way.

Of all her children Bess was emotionally closest to her daughter Mary. Mary was darkly handsome, with sharp, determined features, and shared her mother's spirit if not her prudence. Bess wrote to her with great affection: 'My good sweet daughter, I am very desirous to hear how you do. I trust your Lord is well now of the gout and I desire to hear how all ours do at London and the little sweet Lord Maltravers. I pray God ever to bless you dear heart.' She passed on titbits of gossip, complained of her rheumatism (a rare instance of ill-health), made worse by the 'moist weather' and asked after the children. They are the mundane, loving letters of a mother. Mary's loyalties, however, were as fierce as the temper she shared with her husband and after Shrewsbury's death she became embroiled in Gilbert's feud with Bess. Relations between the new and the dowager Countess suffered a further blow and were temporarily severed when Mary became the confidante and champion of Bess's errant granddaughter, Arbella.

'Paid for hewing 200 foot of window stuff for the highing of 8 windows for two of the turrets.' So reads the entry in the building accounts for April 1594. The turrets, Hardwick's crowning glory, were in place, but it was deemed necessary, presumably on aesthetic and possibly competitive grounds, that their windows and hence the turrets themselves be raised by five feet. It was a decision

taken by Bess but, as she was at Chatsworth, imple-
mented by John Balechouse. By November the roof was
completed and work became concentrated on Hardwick's
interiors. Stone was cut for 'lonng steappes' for the stairs.
John Marker, a plasterer, was paid for nails to 'nayl up
braddets for his cornish' in the long gallery. In May 1596
William Bramley, the joiner, panelled Bess's withdrawing
chamber. The plastering, the glazing and the privies were
finished by the summer of 1597 and in September, in a
final flurry of activity, Bramley panelled the great hall and
the window alcoves in Bess's bed chamber. Hardwick was
habitable. On 4 October Bess was triumphantly played
into her new house by four musicians.

National Trust Photo Library/Geoff Morgan

Hardwick Hall, Derbyshire

The finest portrait of Bess (thought to be a copy of a Nicholas Hilliard original by his apprentice, Rowland Lockey) shows her in old age, dressed in black taffeta with a widow's cap and a starched ruff. Her sole ornament is her five-stranded rope of pearls (these were extremely costly and thus highly prized; on one occasion Bess gave Arbella £100 to buy a single pearl). Her features are little altered by time, but her expression has hardened and she fixes the observer with a penetrating, sardonic eye.

Still vigorous at 70, Bess largely spent her days in her bed and withdrawing chambers, close to the room occupied by Arbella, who had moved into Hardwick with her. In her withdrawing chamber, hung with the tapestries she had bought in London from Sir William Hatton, she had a chair of gilded black leather, with a footstool, a small chair of gold cloth with a gold and red silk fringe, five stools of 'turkie worke', a screen covered with violet cloth edged with black lace and cushions of gold and red damask. An inventory of furnishings made in 1601 gives just some idea of the glowing russets, crimsons, purples and golds with which Hardwick's light-flooded interiors were draped and cushioned. Hangings, cushion covers and table carpets were exquisitely embroidered with allegories, emblems and the ever-present ES's by Bess and her ladies (and at least one full-time embroiderer was kept on the staff). Some still exist. What has vanished, melted down in the civil wars of the 17th century, is Bess's vast collection of plate. Her accounts record a steady accumulation of standing cups, basins and ewers, spoons, flagons, platters and bowls, candlesticks and sconces. Some of these were gifts, to family – Mary Talbot when she was still in favour received a 'crystall cupe rymed with gould' and a 'great gilt standing cup' – or to friends. The remainder shimmered and shone throughout Hardwick.

A mini-Court revolved around Bess, whose rituals were shaped and indeed enforced by Hardwick's stratified interior. The ground floor was the domain of the servants: the upper servants, drawn from the gentry, had rooms in the Old Hall but used the New Hall's low great chamber for eating and as a kind of common-room; the lower servants, almost all male apart from nursemaids and laundresses, ate in the great hall and slept within shouting distance all over the house – on landings, in passages, outside bedrooms – on pallets or truckle beds that folded into chests. The first floor was where Bess and her family had their rooms, while the top floor was given over to the state rooms.

Bess breakfasted lightly if at all on manchet – a white bread – and beer. Dinner was served at 11am and supper at 5 or 6pm. When dining alone she ate in her withdrawing chamber, but on formal occasions meals were served according to strictly prescribed and elaborate ceremony in the high great chamber on the top floor. Here, beneath the brilliantly coloured and fantastical plaster frieze showing the goddess Diana and her court seated amid forest and exotic beasts (Diana symbolised Elizabeth I, who failed to appreciate this compliment and disappointed Bess by never visiting Hardwick), Bess sat in her 'chare of nedlework with golde and silke frenge', with her guests on richly upholstered stools. Food, rapidly cooling under icy draughts, passed from the kitchens through the great hall, where the lower servants stood to attention, and up the winding stone stairs in a procession led by an usher who carried a rod and called for silence with the words 'Speak softly my masters'. On a table covered with two carpets and damask cloths were placed platters of meat, especially mutton and venison, fish and 'sallats', which were washed down with beer and wine. What Bess could not provide herself had to be bought in (William Jenkinson, a servant, was sent to Hull to buy dried fruits, hops, salt, salad oil and claret). After the main part of the meal came the 'banquet', a kind of dessert course, eaten in a banqueting room, which at Hardwick was in one of the turrets. Before spectacular views Bess and her guests sampled sugary delicacies (sugar was an expensive luxury): 'comfits' (seeds, spices and fruits covered with sugar), 'suckets' (preserved fruits), fancy biscuits, sweet-meats, and jellies made from boiled calves' feet and flavoured with sugar, spices and wine.

Bess's bed chamber, a modest-sized room, doubled as her office and counting-house. Here, marking time by an hour-glass, she could write letters, stash rents in her coffers and, gazing out across the Derbyshire dales falling away beneath her, reflect on the satisfactions of owner-ship. Besides her bed were a cupboard, a folding table, a chair of 'russet sattin stript with silver', several stools, three leather-covered desks (these would have been portable), a mirror, a great iron chest, three large chests, two small ones and eight coffers. In a tiny room off the bedroom stood Bess's 'close stool' – a kind of luxury chamber pot with a hinged lid, a leather seat and three pewter basins – tastefully disguised in blue and white cloth with a red and black silk fringe. In fine weather she could stroll in the gardens, walled but undeveloped; in wet she paced the 116 feet of the long gallery. She would have chatted to Arbella and her gentlewoman servants over embroidery and cards. Sometimes there was music. These were the limited occupations available to an Elizabethan noblewoman. Bess, however, as queen of Derbyshire and possessor of huge estates, had carved a role of her own which brought a whirl of activity, admin-istration and responsibility. Bills had to be paid and sent out, money given to the poor who gathered every week at Hardwick's gates, rents received, land bought, accounts checked, constant legal suits expensively settled, and gifts of money made to her children and Arbella (Bess was generous to her family, but cash handouts were of course a useful means of control). There were further building projects: a banqueting house in the garden, stables, fish-ponds, and almshouses for 12 poor in Derby.

In the 1590s heavy rains and the cost of the continuing war against Spain brought famine and rising prices. Bess's revenues were merely dented. And she kept on acquiring. She pursued her practice of lending money (in the absence of banks, ready cash was a precious com-modity in Elizabethan England and moneylenders a much-maligned necessity, so Bess offered the respectable face of usury), often to Derbyshire neighbours on the security of land. The Earl of Cumberland mortgaged his lands at Edensor, near Chatsworth, to her for £2,050; she bought the manors of Stainsby, Heath and Oldcotes (the site of her new house) from Edward Savage for £3,416; she paid another neighbour, Hercules Foljambe, £1,500 for land; she bought a collection of vicarages from the Queen for £12,750.

Who would inherit such assets naturally excited much speculation. In 1601 Bess drew up her will, eight extremely large and densely written vellum pages. To William, the principal beneficiary, was left the contents of the Old and New Hardwicks, while those of Chatsworth went to Henry (on whom the house was entailed). Bess's servants received £1,000 and the occupants of her almshouses a mourning gown and an annual stipend of 20 shillings. There were bequests to her grandchildren and sums of money for relatives to buy mourning rings. To the Queen went £200 to buy a gold cup; to her eldest daughter, Frances Pierrepont, a book which Bess's best-loved husband, Sir William Cavendish, had had made for her, set with gold and precious stones, 'with her father's picture and mine drawn in it'; to Arbella, £1,000, a splendid 'cristal glass trimmed with silver gilt and set with lapis lazuli and agates', her two sables with gold enamelled heads and her pearls. Arbella, however, was about to forfeit her place in Bess's affections.

By 1602 the 'dearest jewel', at 27 and still living with her grandmother, was looking a little tarnished. It was Arbella's curse to find herself the focus of Catholic plots to depose Elizabeth (and later James I). By far the strongest contender for the English throne was James VI of Scotland, but after James the only claimants were Katherine Grey's son, Lord Beauchamp, and Arbella, both great, great grandchildren of Henry VII. Lord Beauchamp's legitimacy was unproven. Arbella, who could be furnished with a Catholic husband, remained their best hope. There had been recent kidnapping alarms. Bess had written to Burghley to assure him that, 'Arbell walks not late, at such time as she shall take any air, it shall be near the house and well attended on. She goes not to anybody's house at all, I see her almost every hour in the day, she lyeth in my bed chamber.'

At Bess's insistence, for reasons of security, Arbella slept in her grandmother's room. Already overcrowded and with the addition of Bess's towering presence, it must have felt very claustrophobic indeed. Two more polarised personalities could hardly be imagined: where Bess was wont to exercise her mind with accounts or legal papers, Arbella favoured a little Hebrew or Greek; where Bess was circumspect, Arbella was impulsive; where Bess under pressure rose to the occasion, Arbella teetered on hysteria. As with Shrewsbury, Bess misjudged a character whose passions – irrational and uncontrolled – were quite alien to her own. Arbella complained that Bess had threatened to take away her money and jewels, that she was subjected to 'despiteful and disgraceful words' and that she disliked 'being bobbed and her nose played withal'. She was effectively a prisoner at Hardwick.

Having resolved to spring herself free, she launched her campaign with a proposal of marriage. Her intended was Edward Seymour. She could hardly have alighted on a less suitable candidate. Seymour, a youth of 16 whom Arbella had never set eyes on, was another descendant of Henry VII. An act passed by Henry VIII in 1536 forbade those of royal blood to marry without royal consent. A match between Arbella and Seymour created a double dose of royal blood and hence, as doubly threatening to the Queen, made such consent extremely unlikely. And if Arbella required further warning of the consequences of marrying a Seymour she needed to look no further than the sad fate of Katherine Grey, sister to Jane Grey, who, for secretly marrying Edward Seymour's grandfather, the Earl of Hertford, had found herself, along with her husband, incarcerated in the Tower. She died in 1568, alone and still in captivity, having given birth to two sons. Arbella was a romantic and this tale of doomed love, far from warning her off, seemed to exert an irresistible lure (she was drawn to the Seymours not once but twice in her life and the second time with fatal results).

To put her plan into motion Arbella needed help. Having unsuccessfully appealed to James Starkey, the chaplain at Hardwick, she approached John Dodderidge, a trusted servant of Bess's, who reluctantly agreed to broach the subject of marriage and deliver a message to the Earl of Hertford: his grandson Edward was to come to Hardwick in disguise, accompanied by an old man, on the pretext of selling land (this being bait, Arbella calculated, that Bess would be unable to resist). At

Christmas 1602 Dodderidge set off for London. He was not well received. The Earl of Hertford promptly alerted Sir Robert Cecil (Lord Burghley's son and heir) and Dodderidge was marched off to the Gatehouse jail. There was consternation at Court; clearly all was not well at Hardwick. Sir Henry Bronker, a Queen's Commissioner with a reputation for tact, was dispatched to investigate.

Bess was walking in the long gallery, with Arbella, when Sir Henry arrived at Hardwick. Being ignorant of her granddaughter's schemes, she must have viewed his sudden appearance with alarm. Bronker, drawing Bess to one end of the gallery, gave her a letter from the Queen and at the other set about interviewing Arbella who began by denying everything and then partially admitted the truth. Bronker asked her to write a confession. The results were 'confused, obscure and in truth ridiculous', and Bronker concluded that 'her wits were somewhat distracted either through fear of her own grandmother or conceit of her own folly'. She had reason to be fearful. Bronker reported that Bess, anxious that the Queen would hold her responsible for Arbella's perfidy, was 'wonderfully afflicted' and 'took it so ill as with much ado she refrained her hands'.

Bronker departed bearing a letter of incoherent apology from Arbella to the Queen. Bess wrote too, also apologetic, on her granddaughter's behalf, but more crisply. Could, she asked, 'this inconsiderate young woman' be 'placed elsewhere' or married off? She had quite lost patience with Arbella's vagaries: 'I have found her to swarve so much from the truth and so vainly led that I cannot give any credit to her.' Bess was now as anxious to be rid of Arbella as Arbella was of Bess. When it came, the Court's verdict was unwelcome to both – the Queen was prepared to overlook the Seymour affair, Arbella must remain at Hardwick and be watched carefully, but not treated like a prisoner.

Arbella turned to fantasy, telling Bess she had a mystery lover, then revealing his identity, farcically, as James VI of Scotland. She sent off volleys of rambling, incoherent letters to Bronker and to relatives, which Bess intercepted and sent to Robert Cecil, who wrote in the margin of one of her more confused missives, 'I think she has some strange vapours to her brain.' Contemporary opinion held Arbella to have lost her wits; more probably there was method to her madness. Bess reported to Cecil that Arbella had gone on hunger strike, that she 'is so wilfully bent that she hath made a vow not to eat or drink in this house at Hardwick or where I am, till she may hear from her Majesty' (judging from her wan appearance, Arbella may qualify as a 16th-century anorexic). Relations between grandmother and granddaughter were rapidly deteriorating, as Arbella described to Bronker. She and one of her cousins had walked in the great chamber for fear of wearing out the mats in the long gallery ('reserved for you Courtiers', she added sourly). After dinner, when she went to receive Bess's blessing, she was met with a 'voley of most bitter and injurious words', whereupon she retreated to her chamber hotly pursued by Bess with her ladies and her son William. Another 'skirmish' ensued. Bess, however, at 75, her appetite for battle flagging, was worn down, complaining that 'a few more weeks as I have suffered will make an end of me'. The end for Bess was still some way off; but it was not so for the Queen, some five years her junior who despite her failing health still declined to nominate a successor. With tension mounting through the country, it suited the Privy Council to have Arbella tucked away out of sight in Derbyshire.

In March 1603 Arbella made a last bid for freedom and turned to her reliably anarchic uncle, Henry Cavendish, who naturally seized on a chance to irritate his mother. A plot was hatched whereby Henry and a local Catholic called Henry Stapleton would abduct Arbella. Bess described the attempt in a letter to Bronker. One afternoon Arbella left the house and walked across the forecourt to Hardwick's gates, where the two Henrys waited. Henry Cavendish was allowed in to speak to his niece, who then attempted to leave but 'was not suffered' (presumably on the orders of Bess, watching from the windows of her withdrawing chamber) and had to content herself with speaking to Stapleton through the gates. Thanks to Bess's cool head there was nothing to be done and the kidnappers retreated. Only afterwards did she learn that some 40 armed men on horseback had been secreted around and about the house. This incident, especially the fact that Stapleton was a 'very wilful Papist', brought Bronker swiftly back to Hardwick. He decided that the situation was taking its toll on Bess, who 'groweth exceeding weary of her charge, beginneth to be weak and sickly and cannot long continue this vexation'. He recommended Arbella's removal.

On 24 March the Queen died and James I, formerly James VI of Scotland, came to the throne (a transition achieved with remarkable smoothness, thanks to some skilful stage-managing on the part of Cecil). James ordered Henry Grey, the 6th Earl of Kent, to temporarily house Arbella, writing to him, 'We are desirous to free our cousin the Lady Arbella Stuart from that unpleasant life which she has led in the house of her grandmother, with whose severity and age she, being a young lady, could hardly agree.' He would not always extend such sympathy to his cousin and in 1610 sent the hapless Arbella to the Tower for secretly marrying William Seymour, the brother of Edward. There she took to her bed and died of 'extreme leanness' five years later. Bess, relieved of her troublesome granddaughter, must have breathed a sigh of relief. She promptly inserted two notes in the margin of her will, disinheriting Arbella and Henry (Henry, denied the contents of Chatsworth, would, as Bess must have known, be unable to afford to live there; in 1609 he sold the house to William for £8,000).

It was left to Bess, 'a lady of great years, of great wealth, of great wit, which yet still remains', as Gilbert Talbot described her, to orchestrate her death as she had her life, while dramas at Court – the discovery of the Main and Bye plots to depose James and put Arbella on the throne, in which Gilbert and Mary Talbot and Henry Cavendish were rumoured to be involved, and later the more serious Gunpowder Plot, in which again Gilbert was implicated – passed her by. Robert Smythson was commissioned to design a magnificent tomb in All Hallows Church, Derby. Her final building project, the almshouses, was completed. She had the satisfaction of seeing her grandchildren make illustrious marriages: Mary Talbot married the Earl of Pembroke in 1604 and Alathea Talbot married the Earl of Arundel two years later. To a degree she made peace with her family. Arbella came to Hardwick in 1605, armed with a letter of recommendation from the King and with the sweetener of a patent for a peerage which she wished to confer on her uncle, William. Bess, initially suspicious of Arbella's motives and affecting surprise at her 'desiring to come to her from whom she had desired so earnestly to come away', was naturally swayed by such an opportunity for honour and advancement for her favourite son and Arbella was forgiven, rewarded with £300 and a gold cup and reinstated in her will. William got his peerage, for £2,000. As Bess grew enfeebled, William became the self-appointed guardian of her death, controlling access to her, throwing his weight around at Hardwick and doing his best to prevent her leaving any last-minute legacies. He did not altogether succeed.

In January 1608, when Bess knew herself to be dying, she decreed that Mary Talbot (who, with Gilbert and Charles Cavendish, had come to Hardwick in December to be reconciled with her mother) was to have the pearl bed that she had shared with William Cavendish at Chatsworth, but that 'she would give no hangings' (this a characteristic tug of the reins). Gilbert reported to Henry Cavendish that Bess ate little and could not walk and noted with irritation that she had left instructions for sheep and cattle to be driven away from a Talbot estate on her death, so as to prevent Gilbert from getting his hands on them. Bess lay cocooned in her feather bed hung with 'scarlet' (the most expensive variety of woollen cloth), edged with silver lace, with a valance embroidered with gold thistles. To exclude the Derbyshire draughts were five curtains of purple 'bayes', two quilts, three pairs of fustian blankets and six Spanish blankets. She was tended by Elizabeth Digby and Mary Cartwright, her ladies-in-waiting, who held her stomach to ease acute abdominal pain.

Throughout the long wintry nights, Bess, her restless mind looking to the future and foreseeing trouble for her heir, the beloved William, 'laye waking thinking of matters that might concern him much and which perhaps he never thought of'. She urged her dutifully hovering son to 'look about him', to ward off the vultures, in the shape of Gilbert and Henry, waiting in the wings. On 2 February her doctor moved into Hardwick. He prescribed a plaster for her back and dosed her with treacle. On 13 February Bess died, probably in her early eighties (her tomb is thought to overestimate her age as 87). As was noted in the National Records of Derby, 'The old Countess of Shrewsbury died about Candelmas... A great frost this year. The witches of Bakewell hanged.'

Her body was drained of blood, disembowelled and embalmed, then sealed in wax and put in a lead coffin. For a long three months she lay in state in the high great chamber, which was swathed, as were the stairs and the hall, in hundreds of yards (£1,584-worth) of black mourning cloth. Hardwick was transformed into a giant shroud for its creator. Bess had left £2,000 to cover the expenses of her funeral, with orders that it 'be not over sumptuous or performed with too much vain and idle charges'.

In the event, however, the funeral held on 4 May *was* a sumptuous affair and Bess was buried with all the pomp and ceremony befitting a Countess. A procession led by a mourning knight wound its way into the black-draped All Hallows church. Behind the coffin carried by six gentlemen and covered in a black velvet pall walked two hooded gentlemen ushers and Mary, Countess of Shrewsbury, flanked by hooded barons. Bringing up the rear were Bess's family (with the exception of Gilbert Talbot and Henry Cavendish, who, excluded from Bess's will, did not attend), servants, the 12 poor from the alms-houses and hired mourning women. Along with future generations of Cavendishes, her body lies buried in a vault beneath Smythson's monument, a suitably splendid construction, where Bess's painted and crowned effigy lies framed by marble columns, prancing Hardwick stags, gilded lion heads and a panoply of heraldry.

According to Derbyshire myth, Bess would cheat death as long as she continued to build. The winter of 1608 was exceptionally cold. The Thames froze solid as, so the story goes, did the water used by Bess's builders to mix mortar, whereupon she struggled from her bed, drove to the site and ordered boiling ale to be substituted for water, but in vain. And so she drew her last breath. The fact that there was probably no actual building in progress in 1608 is immaterial: myths are born of psychological not literal truths. The sentiment is correct. Building was Bess's lifeblood. From Bess came the vast estates and wealth of the Devonshires (a survey commissioned by William and Charles Cavendish found each in possession of 100,000 acres in 1627). Her descendants are scattered through the English aristocracy: the Dukes of Devonshire, Newcastle, Portland and Kingston; the Earls of Manvers, Pembroke, Kent and Arundel. But her greatest legacy is her only surviving house, the inspirational Hardwick. The inscription on her monument commemorates her fittingly enough as 'Haec inclitissima Elizabetha Salopiae comitissa aedium de Chatsworth, Hardwick et Oldcotes, magnificentia clarissimarum fabricatrix' ('This very celebrated Elizabeth Countess of Shrewsbury built the houses of Chatsworth, Hardwick and Oldcotes, highly distinguished by their magnificence').

BIBLIOGRAPHY

Airs, M: *The Tudor and Jacobean Country House: A Building History* (1998)

Durant, DN: *Bess of Hardwick – Portrait of an Elizabethan Dynast* (1977)

Girouard, M: *Robert Smythson and the Architecture of the Elizabethan Era* (1966)

Handover, PM: *Arbella Stuart* (1951)

Rowse, AL: *The England of Elizabeth* (1950)

Sim, A: *Food and Feast in Tudor England* (1997)

Somerset, A: *Elizabeth I* (1991)

Strickland, A (ed): *Letters of Mary Queen of Scots* (1842)

Weir, A: *Elizabeth the Queen* (1998)

Williams, EC: *Bess of Hardwick* (1959)

Kate Hubbard lives in London and Dorset. She works as a book reviewer and as a reader for Bloomsbury Publishing.